Here's How

Succeed in High School

BARBARA MAYER

NTC LearningWorks
NTC/Contemporary Publishing Company

Library of Congress Cataloging-in-Publication Data
is available from the United States Library of Congress.

Cover illustrations by Art Glazer

Published by NTC LearningWorks
An imprint of NTC/Contemporary Publishing Company
4255 West Touhy Avenue, Lincolnwood (Chicago), Illinois 60646-1975 U.S.A.
Copyright © 1992 by NTC/Contemporary Publishing Company
Printed in the United States of America
International Standard Book Number: 0-8442-2478-2

18   17   16   15   14   13   12   11   10   9   8   7   6   5   4   3   2   1

Dedication

For David,
And for all other teens
who have the good sense
to believe in themselves

Contents

Foreword

How to Succeed in High School should be required reading for every young person before they enter those hallowed halls. Barbara Mayer, an experienced high school teacher and counselor, explores a wide range of issues from improving grades to peer pressure. She speaks as a wise older sister, giving advice that always stresses the value of being your own person, and making your own decisions. She understands the challenges to today's student and, through the interactive strategy of asking questions to be answered by the reader, personalizes each topic.

The message is clear. High school is the big job of the student. It is there for developing the total person—a time to risk, to make mistakes, and to learn and grow. It is an opportunity to establish the foundation for making life what you want it to be. She states, "If high school is a time for learning, which it certainly is, then one of the biggest lessons you can learn before that diploma is tucked under your arm is a solid faith in your own worth as a person.''

This book is not one to be read and cast aside. It is meant to be a reference to guide the emerging adult through the maze of growing up. The wise parent will also profit from reading this book as a way to better understand the challenges facing their children. Ms. Mayer has truly captured the essence of the high school years and has offered a practical guide for living them successfully.

Nancy S. Perry, M.S. Ed., NCC, NCSC
President
The American School Counselor Association

Introduction

How to Succeed in High School discusses many of the problems you face as a teen. No punches are pulled. You deserve all the good advice you can get, and you will find it in this book.

These are not easy days for anyone, with the shadow of war behind us and an uncertain future ahead. The many dangers that seem to find their special prey in teenagers require you to grow up quickly and develop inner strength.

Whether you are new to the high school scene, or well on your way toward graduation, this book has a lot to offer. More than getting through high school successfully, these pages give you a chance to learn more about yourself. They are full of help on how to understand yourself better, and they give you many opportunities to face your own feelings and thoughts as you analyze situations, attitudes, and problems that concern you.

This book doesn't involve regular homework. But it

does include some exercises designed to help you get to know yourself better. The topic of the book isn't anything else but *you*, and all the challenges and opportunities you face. It's full of ways to help you realize the great successes you can achieve.

This is a book, however, and not a television channel. It involves some work on your part. Working your way through this book is worth it, though, since the reward is a more aware, confident, together you!

Read carefully, and learn as much as you can about who you are. Then you can succeed at the art of living as the best teenager and young adult you can be.

Barbara Mayer

Understanding Yourself | 1

If Kermit the Frog feels it isn't easy being green, you may take heart in the fact that it isn't easy being a teen, either. There you sit—a special and unique teenager. What makes you so special? For one thing, by picking up this book you have admitted two very good things about yourself:

1. You want to know more about yourself, and

2. You have at least a vague desire to make your life during these high school years a better one.

You are saying, "Teach me something new," and that makes you one of the healthiest and potentially most terrific people around!

Many people complain about high school, but most sane people will admit that it is an interesting and consequential part of anyone's life. During these four years, you will be asked to make as many decisions as a United Nations member does in the same time period. You will probably do as much work as a U.N. member, too, and you may have to listen to more boring speeches!

Your high school years are a time when you, and many aspects of your life, are changing. These are the years when the adult "you" begins to take definite form. By the time you pick up that diploma and head for your first graduation party, the world will expect that you are capable of handling most jobs, most problems, and most responsibilities of adult life.

That's a tall order. So as you sit down to try to make the most of these three or four years, the first place to begin is getting to know and appreciate yourself. You're not a carbon copy of your brothers or sisters. You're not what your parents think you are. You're not even what your best friend thinks you are.

And even the "real you" is changing as you become an adult. Each decision you make now contributes a great deal to the person you're becoming.

You are on your way; now it's a matter of living the next few years as well as you can.

The Beauty of Being Human

One sure thing you have on your side as you tackle teenage life is the fact you are human. Everyone makes mistakes, has emotions and dreams, and shares the same concerns about living. Circumstances change at different ages, but the one thing all adults must realize about you is that you are basically good, as they are. You have potential and ambition, as they do, and you share the same faults and possible talents.

The problem for many teens is simply understanding these facts themselves. Adolescence is a pressure-packed time. The very word sounds more like a disease than a time of life. Parents and teachers seem to keep addressing the matter of success or failure, and teens can get so caught up in the hassle of meeting requirements that they forget to pay attention to their own humanity.

Facing the high school years becomes much easier if you understand yourself. Others may set goals for you and expect certain things from you, but you must be true to yourself. You're the one who has the task of making the most of yourself and your future.

No small change

One of the first things to understand about yourself is that you are changing. A lot of adults, and some who may be making your life miserable, have never really understood that life moves. Times and people change. Part of the human condition is to move and change, too.

The world of nature has evolved over millions of years. Chickens, scientists say, used to have large wings. Modern chickens have no use for them, however, and the wing has slowly become an insignificant part of the chicken's body. Just try making a meal of one chicken wing!

People also evolve during their lifetimes. There are many things you did and felt as a child. Now they are inconsequential because your life has moved into a different, more complex stage. One great secret which you should begin to understand is that this evolutionary process is still going on, and will continue as long as you live.

Rapping It Up

The first important concept in understanding yourself is to recognize and be comfortable with your own personal development.

Others in your life may not be so quick to notice and respond to the changes. Parents are notorious for not realizing their children have reached a certain age and a certain level of development. Just when your folks have learned to cope with you at fourteen, your fifteenth birthday has rolled around, and you are already moving on to new levels of awareness and maturity. This, of course, is one of the causes of the famous communication gap.

One simple answer is to recognize and respond to the changes inside yourself. Once you are sure of these changes, it is easier for other people in your life to be aware of them, too.

Points to Ponder

1. What do you consider your most important change over the past year?

_____

_____

Why is it so important to you?

_____

_____

2. What changes in yourself do you feel others have failed to notice?

   _____

   _____

   Why do you think this has happened?

   _____

   _____

3. What is important to you now that wasn't very important last year at this time?

   _____

   _____

   What do you think this change says about you?

   _____

   _____

4. At this point, name two things which may be keeping you from really liking yourself.

   _____

   _____

Values and Priorities

Social studies teachers are famous for requiring students to learn who discovered what, and when. Knowing such facts may make your report card less traumatic and win some points on the home front, but the most important discovery you can make during your teens is who you are, and who you are becoming.

"Great," you say. "But how can I do it?"

First, look at the things that are important in your life. What you value, what is high on your list of priorities, says a lot about you. What gives you pleasure? Is it having a closet full of clothes and the best sound equipment this side of Jupiter? Is it your family? Is it knowing you have good friends who can be trusted and who will be there when you need them? Is it taking a quiet walk by yourself and just listening to the world going by? What is most important to you—making the honor roll or hanging out with your friends?

Although you may not want to take the time to do it, you

should calmly sit down and make a list of the things you value. It will give you a fairly good idea of who you are now, and who you're possibly becoming. True, there are many facets to your life at this point, and they all need attention. But what you value most will take your best effort and most of your time. By looking at where you are putting your energy, you can begin to realize certain directions your life is taking. That realization will give you a better understanding of yourself.

Believing Is Seeing

What you believe is also a key factor in your identity. And the other side of that coin is just as important. What you choose not to believe will affect the way you respond to many circumstances that come along. It will set patterns that may last throughout the rest of your life.

For example, if your religious beliefs are important to you, many decisions you make will find their source in these convictions. If, on the other hand, you are not strongly influenced by religion, you may have to look for other areas of security. You may need to find some working alternatives for religious guidelines and principles of living.

If you feel loved by your family, home and family responsibilities may be important to you. Or, getting out of the house may be one of your most sought-after pleasures, and the time you spend there may often be filled with tension and frustration. If so, you should be aware that your own attitudes toward marriage and family life may be developing in negative ways.

If you have trouble honestly loving the people who have shared all of your life with you, you may have to set some priorities straight and get things back into perspective before you launch out to find the one and only who will "really understand." What you believe and what you love are two of the most basic things about you. By honestly analyzing these two aspects of your life, you can learn a lot about yourself and begin to make any changes you think are in order.

Decisions! Decisions!

Another tip-off to your own identity lies in looking at the choices you make. There is only so much time in each day, and you have limited energy. What you decide to do, or not do, stems directly from your values and priorities, and shows you the direction in which you are headed.

If making the honor roll is the be-all and end-all of your

life, and your parents demand nothing less than A's, you often may find yourself putting in some extra study time instead of taking a few hours to do things you would enjoy more. The pressure for grades is intense for some teens, and because of it, some students neglect other aspects of their lives.

Work is fine. It is part of the human condition and should be a serious concern in everyone's life. When, however, the need to succeed in one area begins to overshadow the greater success that comes from being a well-rounded and balanced person, it is time to realign priorities and learn to keep things in perspective. Putting all your apples in one cart may sound like a good idea, but the world does not live by apple pie alone!

You may be smiling at this point. "Never fear," you say. "Don't worry about me spending too much time with the books!" You may even be so caught up in your "cool" image at school that you won't volunteer the right answer when you know it, just so others won't think you're an egghead.

In this case, once again, the decisions and choices you make are yours. They tell you, and the rest of the world, what you care about, what you are, and what you want to be. They also tell you how much importance you place on other people's opinions of you.

Your Place in the Group

Another good way to understand more about who you really are, is to analyze how you react to most situations.

Imagine a teacher who sets up a group project in class and turns several students loose on a particular topic. The project calls for some understanding of basic principles, some ideas to set it going, and then some action.

As soon as the group gets settled, Steve immediately starts talking. He begins to set things in motion. He is a natural leader, and when something needs to get done, he takes charge and gets everyone else working. He is the spark plug, the initiator, and because of his intangible leadership quality, others follow him. Even though they may challenge him on certain points, they accept him as the person in charge.

Julie, on the other hand, sits back a while. She is the thinker. While everyone else is busy getting preliminary discussion out of the way, she is quietly sizing up the big picture. When her time comes, she may say very little, but her ideas are the most workable. The suggestions she makes form the basis for the whole project.

Once the work begins, Ed will jump in, volunteering to handle one aspect of the project. He may not be the person who comes up with the ideas, but he is a doer. Where he shines is in taking the ball and running with it. Because he may not be sure enough of himself to propose new ideas, Ed is a follower. He is the one who does most of the actual work, and he does it well. Once he understands where the project is going, he sets his own goals and does the work necessary to achieve them. People like Ed are often the ones who succeed in the future.

Over on the fringe of the group sits Kathy. Ah, Kathy! At this point in her life, Kathy is still very much a spectator. She is too unsure of herself and her abilities to really succeed, so she chooses to stay in the background. She watches others participate, and she avoids any possible confrontations. Kathy's time will come eventually, and she will become involved in the project when others demand it. Her choice, however, is to remain on the sidelines and let everyone else handle things.

What would you do if you were part of this group? Are you a natural leader like Steve, or are you more like Kathy? Notice how you act in group situations, and you will have another important clue to your true self.

Try to remember the last time you took part in a group activity. Now try to decide if you are an achiever, a leader, an idea person, a follower, or a key worker. Write your answer here, and be able to talk about your reasons.

_____

_____

_____

_____

_____

The "In" Crowd

Kathy is not the only one who may choose to sit back and spectate. There is another type of person who may sit on the sidelines, simply because that's where he or she feels safe. As high school groups and cliques develop—and they certainly will—one group of students becomes the "in" clique in school. While a certain amount of popularity is great, and everyone needs friends, some members of the "in" clique develop some strange characteristics.

Some of the people in this group become so secure in their popularity that they feel they never have to try for anything. They may be physically attractive, or they may have personalities that win over teachers and authority figures. What can happen to them, however, is that they get everything too easily. They don't really *do* anything; they just *are* popular. They may be chosen homecoming king or queen, be on the prom court, and have their pictures all over the yearbook.

But some of these students don't really work hard at anything; they have a tendency to let any group down when work needs to be done. Why? They don't know how to follow a project through because they've never had to do it. As a result, they add their presence to your group, but little more.

A bit hard on popular people? Maybe. But it's often true. And sadly, some high school superstars don't succeed much after high school. They get in the groove of simply being part of the right crowd and using that popularity as success. In later life, when work and the ability to follow through are essential to getting and keeping a good job, these people are often missing many of the basic skills others learned the hard way in high school. Don't let yourself use popularity as a substitute for hard work.

Of course, many popular people do find lasting success. The answer is simply not being satisfied with knowing you're on the inside, where most others would love to be. Learn to work and follow through, and you can achieve goals that last far beyond the fleeting high school years.

Roles Aren't Everything

Our world has become very specialized and role-oriented. When two strangers meet, one of the first questions usually is, "What do you do?" What we do, our job, seems to be an easy way for others to put us in perspective. While this is all right to a degree, there is a great danger of confusing our different roles with our basic identities.

As a teenager, you are cast in many different roles. You may be a son or daughter, a friend, a student, a brother or sister, a teammate, a club member. Each of these roles is good and is something which makes certain demands on you; each brings its own rewards and happiness.

When it comes to understanding your true self, however, it's easy to get *what* you are confused with *who* you are. Each role exists because of circumstances in your life, and because life changes, these roles also will change. Some will disappear as others take their place. You will not be a student forever, but you may be an employee, a husband or wife, or a parent. If you define and understand yourself only in terms of the roles in your life, there will be little room left for your own security and sense of yourself. Then the really beautiful aspects of your personality may go unnoticed.

Understanding yourself means going beyond the exteriors and the different roles you fill. Until you know *who* you really are, *what* you are can become frustrating and confusing.

A Self-Inventory

Check the characteristics that you feel best describe you.

___ Shy	___ Good listener
___ Leader	___ Take charge
___ Creative	___ Dreamer
___ Follower	___ Friendly
___ Accurate	___ Achiever
___ Talkative	___ Producer
___ Sociable	___ Need acceptance
___ Demanding	___ Precise
___ Neat	___ Loner

Which adjectives did you choose to describe yourself? Select one adjective, and give an example of a time when your behavior illustrated that characteristic. (Example: If you described yourself as shy, you may recall a time when you wanted to give an answer in class or introduce yourself to someone at a party, but you didn't speak up.) Write your answer below:

Characteristic: _____

Example: _____

_____

Don't Worship Images   Similar to the concept of role is the concept of image. In every school students are categorized by some image they project. Because of this, there is great danger of living up to one's image, rather than one's true identity.

People tend to like things neat and simple. No one likes to be unsure of things. As a result, it is easy to put each person we meet into some kind of pigeonhole, a neat category. Steve is an athlete; Debbie is a dropout; Mike is class president. This system is simple, but is it healthy? Never!

Everyone longs for acceptance and appreciation from others. Your friends help meet those needs. And, as the months go by, you are probably getting at least enough positive response from others to make life bearable. Part of that popularity, however, may stem from an image which you have managed to establish, and here the real danger lurks. You may begin to see that image of yourself as the real you.

No one has much respect for the teacher who is so caught up with his image as the boss that he forgets to be human. It's easy to see he has a problem. But then, it is always easy to see other people's problems. Identifying these same characteristics in ourselves, however, may take a bit more work.

Since no one likes living up to an image all the time, one solution is to start respecting others' individuality. Sure, they may belong to a particular group, and have certain kinds of friends, but beginning to take people for what they honestly are is a way of beginning to see yourself honestly, too. No matter how great someone's image may be, it is only a hollow shell, a false front. There are no great images. There are only great people.

Your life-style and your present job as a student are part of your life. What you do for entertainment, how you see the need to be extremely popular, the need to include drugs or alcohol as an essential part of entertainment, and the way you choose to look and dress are aspects of your life. But they are not the real you. By getting caught up in what we think the world expects of us, and giving in to the pressures we feel, we may give a super impression on the outside. Where it really counts, however, there may be nothing but disaster. Living in a mold we or someone else has created may make life easier for a while, but it is usually a mistake in the long run.

Rapping It Up   What are you really all about, anyway? For starters, as a teenager you are a person in the no-man's land between childhood and adulthood. You are dynamic because of your thirst for a fuller life, because your goals are high, and your potential is great. You are a person on the move, a changer, an innovator. You haven't gotten into the habit of settling for second best, and you know things can be better.

By understanding that you, too, are on your way to becoming better, you can build a real respect and honest appreciation of your own worth. By looking at your own responses and decisions, you can evaluate your life as it is. By looking at your own ability for success and your distaste for failure, you can realize the possibilities you can achieve.

Be calm and comfortable with yourself. Understand that you, as a unique individual, are more than a number on a computer card in the high school office. You are special. No image or mold could possibly contain all you really are. By facing *what* and *who* you are already, you can set yourself well on the way to a fuller and richer life. Only you will set the limits you decide to accept.

Be good to yourself, and learn to smile at that mirror once in a while. The person you see there is your best friend. When you really like him or her, nothing can stop you.

Points to Ponder

1. List the three most important things in your life. Why are they so special to you?

   _____

   _____

2. Name one decision you made recently. What does it tell about your values?

   _____

   _____

3. How does people's image of you differ from what you really are?

   _____

   _____

4. Think back to one of your recent failures. What do you think was the major cause of this setback?

   _____

   _____

What Is High School All About?

While it may be normal to say you hate school as much as you like spring break, there remains another reality. Many teenagers learn to really enjoy their high school years.

A Fact of Life   School is a very basic fact of your life right now, and once you can get beyond the stage of living up to images and stereotypes, school can become a place where you really enjoy yourself. One of the basic principles for enjoying anything is first to understand it, recognize its value, and then learn how to cope with any problems it may bring.

Basically, the purpose of high school is to provide you with the opportunity to learn and develop to your maximum potential. Academics are important, but only the beginning of what high school can offer. You may win every science award available and still be miserable if you don't know how to live fully and comfortably with yourself and others. If you gain all the knowledge and skill necessary to be a computer programmer, and cannot deal with fellow workers, you won't get very far! So participating in classes and passing tests are not enough to make your high school years a success or to prepare you for the future. Let's take a good look at some of the skills that are also part of learning.

A,B,C, Plus You and Me

The academic subjects—English, Social Studies, Math, and all the rest—are not really intended as instruments of torture. Educators often reexamine what they teach to keep the material relevant and up-to-date. And once they determine that certain forms of knowledge and skills are definite requirements in society, they have an obligation to help you learn them. As the world shrinks and more competition comes from graduates all over the globe, schools must keep grade requirements high and stress mastery of essential skills.

We will be talking more about teachers later, but let's just say for now that no good teacher will challenge you unrealistically and defy you to pass his or her class. Real education is not a battle of wits, where the teachers are the bad guys, trying to outsmart the good guys, who, naturally, are the students. True learning should be the goal of any good school system, and when teachers fail to present material in a meaningful way, it is the school's fault, not the student's.

The word education comes from the Latin word *educare*. This word does not mean pouring facts into a person's head. It means "pulling or drawing out." Real education, then, is not pouring facts into your brain. It is drawing out all the talent and potential that is in you. Presenting the required knowledge is the job of the school. Learning as much as is individually possible is the duty of each student.

Some subjects may not seem useful to you. English, for example, may not seem that important now. However, when the time comes to write to that terrific person you met last summer, or when you have a job interview the next day, you may wish you had paid more attention to the finer points of the language. Math can be a drag at times. Yet when your checkbook balances, and you can compute figures in finance and start estimating percentages for taxes and profit, math can become not only an ally, but a real source of pleasure.

Skills are as important as subjects

What many teens fail to realize during their education is that the skills they use during school are as important as the material covered on tests. Not everyone is going to remember all the facts and bits of knowledge teachers put in exams. But skills—such as learning how to study and how to plan—will never be forgotten.

Learning how to use the library and react intelligently to newspapers, magazines, and television may not seem important when you are learning these things. When you are out of school, however, and all of your knowedge must come from the media and other sources, those weeks of tearing apart commentators' opinions and rummaging through the school library will begin to pay off.

People 101

There is no class called "People 101." Yet one of the most valuable forms of knowledge a high school can offer is just that—learning about people.

The step from a smaller elementary or junior high school into a large high school is, for some, traumatic. There are so many people, so many strange faces, and so many different things people are doing! But that exposure to all kinds of people and all kinds of opinions and life-styles can teach you some of the most important lessons you learn.

Dealing with people your own age isn't always easy. Some will demand more than you are ready to give. Some will ridicule you for your beliefs and your own response to life. Some may question your right to get in the way of their ideas. But by looking honestly at the members of your classes, and then deciding what you do and don't like about them, you can begin to get a broader idea of the kinds of people you will meet in the years after school. You can learn to choose your friends and deal with others on your own terms.

Watching how other teens deal with their problems can also be a big lesson. There are the "druggies" and the drinkers. Their life-style is clear, and they each have their muddled reasons for using and addiction. They can teach you a lot in a negative way. Theirs is not the answer.

However, you can also learn positive things from fellow

students. A former student once said he was trying to tell a certain girl how he felt about her. His shyness and lack of confidence, however, kept him from being able to carry it off. Then a friend of his, who was a football and baseball player, confided that he had copied a seventeenth century love sonnet they had been studying in English class. He had given the copy to his girlfriend.

This football player may have had a big macho image with everyone else, but he was also his own man. He had no fear of showing his gentle side when it came to the tender things of life.

The student took his example from that friend's courage, and also copied the poem. After slipping it in the girl's notebook, he began what turned out to be a good relationship. Without the courage he gained from his friend's stronger conviction, though, the student might still be sitting in the back of class, worrying about how to approach a girl and not believing in himself.

The Team Approach

Another value of working with people during your high school years is the experience you can get by submerging your own efforts into a group. The teens are years when most young people are trying to find their own individuality. So they can sometimes get so self-involved that they forget they don't have to do everything themselves.

State championships are not usually won by all-stars. The team of players who can make the sacrifice, and give up some of their own glory once in a while for the good of the team, are the ones who win in the end. By working with others in group efforts such as plays, yearbooks and newspapers, clubs, and class projects, you can learn how to deal with different kinds of people. You can also begin to realize you don't always have to work for things alone.

Developing both leadership and teamwork skills is as important a lesson to learn during high school as is writing a good composition or passing math class.

Rapping It Up

School is one of the few places left in our society where what is unknown or sometimes faulty is just as important as that which is positively sure and perfectly correct. Being a student gives you the luxury of being wrong once in a while. If you never made mistakes and knew everything, there would be no need for school.

Take advantage of these years when you are expected to learn by trial and error. Don't be afraid to discard things about yourself or your life that you feel don't fit any more. Yours is the luxury of changing your mind and rearranging your perspective, so go ahead and do it, as long as you are convinced of the worth of your actions and the possible good that can come from them. High school is a time to pick and choose, to learn and develop all that you can, and to form patterns of living and responding that will last a lifetime.

What is high school all about? It's about you! It is about the best possible you—the person who can some day walk away from the teachers, the books, and the circumstances that make this time of your life so exciting and challenging.

School exists for you—not you for it. Remember this, and take the best high school has to offer as you count those months until graduation.

Points to Ponder   1. What is one specific thing you dislike about school?

_____

Is there anything reasonable you do can do about the problem? If so, what? If not, how can you rise above it?

_____

_____

_____

_____

2. What lessons have you learned lately by watching your fellow students and seeing how they do things?

_____

_____

_____

_____

3. How have you changed since this time last year?

_____

_____

_____

_____

4. List some after-school activities that are attractive to you. Why do these activities appeal to you?

_____

_____

_____

_____

Attitude

4

One thing no one can tolerate in this world is injustice. Suppose one student gets caught smoking marijuana and is suspended for the rest of the semester. Another also is nabbed, but is suspended for only three days, then returns to school with all credits and privileges still intact.

"Unfair!"

The cry of injustice can be heard from the gym to the cafeteria, and teens shake their heads and point to the rotten state of fair play and equal treatment in their school.

These situations do occur, and there is a logical explanation for them. There may have been different circumstances surrounding these two particular cases. There also may have been two very different attitudes on the part of the offenders. Many decisions made by administrators and those in authority are influenced by that slippery, intangible thing called attitude. Some people can almost get away with anything because of their attitude and response in times of trouble. Others get hung by their own words because they respond to difficulties by creating more difficulty.

Attitude is really a response. It is the way you deal with life, and it comes from deep inside your personality. Attitude is the basic pattern you have for dealing with people and circumstances, and it has been evolved, along with the rest of you, through your own heredity and the individual world in which you live. If you really like who you are and who you are becoming, you will probably be at ease with your attitude toward people and things. If you are unhappy, your attitude will probably mirror your misery.

Accentuate the Positive

One of the surest ways of ensuring survival, and even success, in high school is beginning with a positive approach. Some teens drag themselves through the school doors every day, dreading every minute they are trapped in that academic jail, and marking off the days until vacation like prisoners awaiting release. These students are only encouraging their own misery and lack of success in school.

Any winning coach will tell you that when the team is convinced they can win, they probably will. Anyone who thinks he can dance well probably will. Positive mental attitude does give you a positive chance at success. Students who set realistic academic goals and then believe they can reach them, will probably surprise even themselves with their success.

Every year awards are given to students and players who have shown good attitude, and bookstores are full of material that tells you how to develop a winning attitude for any aspect of life. The trouble with attitude is that you don't see it. You don't get a grade for it, and just when you think you have it pinned down, it slips away and turns up in a way you never expected. Once controlled, however, it can make you unstoppable!

One Success Story

Attitude, for some strange reason, is a difficult thing for most adults to explain. "I don't like your attitude" is as close as most adults get in discussions with teens. When pressed for a deeper explanation, they might simply say, "Be nice."

What adults are really trying to say is what they have discovered from their successes and failures in life—that an open, positive approach to life, liking yourself and liking the challenges you meet, is the best way to be happy and successful.

Today many advertisers and entertainers seem to make the unhappy scowl part of their act. In many movies and videos, there is a tendency to act like nothing is good, nothing is worth getting excited about, and unhappiness and mistrust are "in." What you have to remember, however, is that all those entertainers are putting on an act. They have a very positive attitude about their work and about the money they make for it, and believing in themselves is part of what allowed them to build successful careers.

A positive attitude and self-confidence can bring you success too. For example, one high school student's extra weight was causing embarrassment and frustration. It was standing in the way of a happier life. Like too many teens, some of her classmates were very cruel to this student. She tried every diet and form of weight reduction, but got no results.

One day something happened. Becoming disgusted with the problem, the student simply decided to lose weight. With her assumption that it would work, the weight began to come off! Her will power and ability to stick to a regimen of proper eating were phenomenal, and by the time it was all over, she lost fifty-five pounds. What emerged from this battle of the bulge was a totally new person, and one who learned she could make things happen by keeping a positive attitude. And because of the self-respect that girl developed, the respect of others followed. By proving that with the proper attitude she could attain seemingly unreachable goals, the student emerged with an entirely new and positive outlook on life.

A positive approach to life, and its many problems, can make a big difference. Many young people, feeling the pressures and demands of school, begin to think the world is out to get them. There seem to be so many obstacles to success, so few rewards, and the challenges never stop coming. Because of this stress, teens can easily develop a negative attitude toward adults, authority figures, and anything that seems not to fit in their present world. Teens who work to maintain a more positive attitude, however, have a much better chance of succeeding in high school.

Inventory

Do you find negative attitudes in your home? In your friends? Give an example.

_____

_____

_____

What brings out a negative attitude in you?

_____

_____

_____

What can you do to control this?

_____

_____

_____

Name a problem or difficult situation you face. List some positive things you could do to solve or improve it.

_____

_____

_____

_____

_____

Chronic Cynicism

One of the greatest illnesses that teens can pick up today is a nasty litle thing called Chronic Cynicism. Maybe television encourages teens to grow up too fast, and provides too many experiences too early. Something, however, has driven some of our best young people into a defensive attitude where they begin to put down just about everything, and pass judgement on anything that crosses their paths.

It may give these teens a false sense of superiority, and it may be their way of fighting back against all the put-downs they have received, but Chronic Cynicism is a personality killer, and it is extremely contagious.

Everyone can think of some adult they know who is bitter, narrow-minded, negative, and cynical. These people are not the world's greatest candidates for Mr. or Miss Personality, and most people avoid them. Most of these miserable specimens, remember, did not become that way overnight. It took years of steady training, and one negative reaction after another to bring these people to their current state. Guess where some of them began? Right! Their teens!

If you or any of your friends feel that horrible illness of Chronic Cynicism creeping up, and it will from time to time, stop. Listen to some of your favorite music. Take a walk. Return a smile. Do anything that will bring the good and positive things of this world back into focus for you.

The Right Attitude Is the Right Approach

Developing the right attitude, then, is one sure way of having a successful, happy high school career, and a lifetime of more of the same. Being open first of all to yourself, and then to others, will make you easier to get along with. It will also make you much more approachable and able to make new friends. Negative and cynical people repel others. But warm and friendly people, who presume the best and who are ready to cope with the worst, are joys to all they meet.

This positive attitude is not unrealistic or sugary. It is possible to be aware of problems and be strong enough to initiate change when necessary, to take the hard knocks of life and still maintain an open, positive attitude.

Rapping It Up

Remember the students who were caught smoking marijuana? Why did one student get the book thrown at him while another got by with a much more lenient punishment?

The student who was expelled for an entire semester had a chip on his shoulder, spoke sarcastically to all authority figures, and thereby invited adults to return his anger with harshness and the worst possible punishment. This student went into the principal's office expecting the worst. He let the principal know he was ready for the worst by his negative and surly attitude, and therefore he got the worst!

The other student approached the principal with open, honest realism. He tried to be sincere, admitting his guilt and expressing regret for getting into trouble. His positive attitude toward punishment and his own failure made the administrator more humane and lenient. This student was granted a chance to see his mistakes, acknowledge them, and grow. The principal also gave this second student lesser punishment.

Your attitude should always be honest and sincere, but it should also be realistic and positive. By approaching your high school career in an open and optimistic manner, you can give yourself a big advantage over others. While some teens waste their time in negativism and bitterness, you can begin to build more positive skills for living by taking each day as it comes, expecting the best, realizing what is happening, and working for improvement.

You may not be the most intelligent person in your school, but nothing can keep you from becoming the most positive!

Points to Ponder

1. How would you rate your attitude toward school? More positive? Or more negative?

   _____

   What is the cause for this?

   _____

   _____

2. Is your attitude toward yourself more negative or positive? Why?

   _____

   _____

   _____

   _____

3. Name one time you showed some Chronic Cynicism.

   _____

   _____

   What caused your cynicism?

   _____

   _____

   _____

4. Can you think of any people you know whose sour attitude ruins their effectiveness with others? What would you say to them if you had the chance?

   _____

   _____

   _____

   _____

   _____

   _____

The Classroom

Students may think of it as a torture chamber. Parents may view it as a battleground. Teachers may see it as a place of confrontation and exhausting effort. In reality, today's high school classroom is one of the most exciting and stimulating places to be.

True, educators have made mistakes. Class offerings have been revised and revised again. But just as you are evolving, education is constantly changing, too. The knowledge is there for the taking, and if you can learn to take advantage of it, you can walk away from high school with a great deal.

With other countries from Japan in the Orient to the new European powerhouse of a united Germany already profiting from strong educational systems, America is now undergoing more change to follow suit. Both business leaders and educators are determined to provide U.S. students with an education that will allow them to compete in the modern world. Training you to learn as much as possible is the goal, and a solid understanding of what goes on in the classroom is your greatest advantage.

Study the Schedule First

Debbie is a junior now. Last month she decided she wanted to go into nursing. A visit to her counselor and a check of her credits, however, revealed some low grades in science and some gaps in the requirements Debbie's school of choice demands. As a result, Debbie may have to take some classes in an adult education program, and she may not be able to enter the nursing school right after graduation. There also is a chance those low science grades may make acceptance to that nursing school questionable.

Of course there is no way any teen can be expected to know at the time first-year schedules are being made exactly what career he or she will pursue. It is, however, possible to keep options open, and to protect your future by doing your best in the basic academic classes.

Choosing the right schedule may seem confusing to first-year students, but counselors are available. With their knowledge of what colleges and specialized schools require, they can give good advice. Many times teens never realize how much help is available, and how easy it is to plan alternative classes.

Most high schools offer elective classes in many different fields. These range from journalism and creative metalworking to stagecraft and business management. Preparing for the future in today's society requires a solid understanding of the basics, but it also helps to explore elective classes for possible occupations or hobbies in the adult world.

One of the best things you can do throughout your high school career is to get to know your counselor. Drop by the office from time to time, check into what is new in requirements and credits, and see how you are progressing. Report cards may be enough to keep your parents happy every few months, but your parents aren't going to live your adult life. If you really intend to get all you can out of the academic experience, some honest talks with your counselor can open up new horizons and new possibilities for your consideration.

Easy Street May Be a Dead End

One temptation for high schoolers, which is often even more inviting if friends choose that path, is the opportunity to sign up for so-called "blow off classes." Every high school has some classes that don't require extensive homework and are considered easy credits. If you are not aware of any of these classes in your school, you've probably not been out of your locker for the past six months.

The best way to choose classes is to look at what your interests are and where you believe you will learn the most. The world is full of adults who admit making the mistake of taking too many easy classes while they were in school. Now they regret passing up opportunities. Many, now enrolled in adult education programs or stuck in dead-end jobs, look at today's high school schedules and wish things had been different for them.

Wasting the opportunities high school offers may not seem important now. However, giving subjects a try before you decide against them may give your life an extra boost you'll appreciate in later years.

Sliding by is always the easiest way to go. The only trouble with it is that you sometimes fall down!

Learn How You Learn Best

One of the greatest problems of education is that it is geared to teaching all students with the same techniques. It presumes all students learn the same way. True, there are accelerated classes for more advanced students, and more basic classes for those who need more help, but *the way* students are taught tends to stay very much the same.

A simple fact recognized lately is that not all students learn best by reading and watching the teacher make hieroglyphics on a chalkboard. Roughly 50 percent of students are eye-minded. They learn by seeing, by reading, and by remembering what they have seen. The traditional educational process is geared to them, with teachers requiring students to read textbooks, copy notes from the board, and write answers on tests. Eye-minded students usually do well in school because they are able to respond to this kind of teaching. They have a definite advantage. If you tend to remember where you saw an ad in a magazine, and even remember what corner of the page it was in, you are probably eye-minded. You're lucky.

An ear-minded person learns best by sound. He or she learns by remembering what the teacher said and will do best in lecture classes. When forced to read the material alone, the person may lose interest and fail to remember key points.

Parents often complain that their children are bright and alert at home, know all the answers when quizzed, but then fail to do well on tests at school. If ear-minded persons were given oral tests they would probably raise their grade averages considerably. Often, however, no one realizes why the ear-minded student is having difficulty. Soon the student begins to think of him- or herself as just not very intelligent. If you have trouble with spelling or are a slow reader, you may be ear-minded.

Students who feel they may be ear-minded should try using tape recorders for important lectures. They should try studying aloud when they can. Talking about the subject matter and discussing it with others are also some of the best learning tools for ear-minded students. Ear-minded people make up about 40 percent of the student body.

The other 10 percent, action-minded people, are at the greatest disadvantage of all in the normal school process. Action-minded students learn best by doing, by working with their hands, by actually holding and handling, and through personal experience with things. The best way action-minded students can cope with school is to write notes and make outlines of important material, complete with pictures. Devising key symbols for main ideas and making diagrams and even cartoons can help impress facts on their minds. When choosing classes, action-minded people would be wise to go heavy on lab classes, where book work is only part of the program, and where it's possible to learn the most by actually doing.

The First Week

Now comes the big question.

"I walk into class on the first day. What do I do? How can I really succeed?"

The first week or two of each semester should be a time of studying and judging. That doesn't mean immediately reading half the textbook and doing enough extra-credit papers to sink a battleship. Those first days should be spent studying the one thing that will determine everything else that happens in that classroom—the teacher.

There is no course on how to study teachers. Your success in any subject, however, will depend heavily on how well you understand the teacher and know what he or she expects from you. First take a look at the teacher as a human being. Does the teacher seem comfortable and at ease with the class, or overly formal? Strict formality is a tip-off that he or she is very image-conscious and will probably run a very tight ship! Is the teacher interested in getting to know the students' names, or does he or she immediately get down to the business at hand and launch into a lecture to end all lectures? If the teacher immediately begins teaching, he or she is probably most concerned with getting the subject matter across, and you may find yourself in an uphill battle if you want to assert your identity in that classroom.

The teachers who try to get to know their students at the beginning of a new class may turn out to be the ones you turn to with a problem or in time of crisis. If you find the teacher encouraging discussion and trying to learn names quickly, you have just signed on with a person who is probably aware of his or her own individuality, and will be encouraging you to find your own all through the semester. This type of teacher will also be one who will want you to give your own opinions on topics that arise, and, in most cases, you can at least expect the teacher to be aware of you as a unique human being.

Studying the personalities of your teachers will give you a good idea of what classes will be like and help you when you must decide who gets your limited study time. By knowing what the instructor will expect, and what he or she feels is important, you can begin to get the class under control in your mind and relieve any pressures you may have felt going into it.

Introduce yourself

"Corny. Very corny! The last thing in the world I want is for the teacher to know me," you might say. "The farther away I can stay, the better off I'll be!"

Not so. Sooner or later your presence will become known in that classroom. If nothing else, you may be absent one day, and the teacher will ask who sits there! The teacher will know who you are, all right, so that argument won't work.

The teacher, though, is confronting over a hundred different students a day. He or she has a certain amount of material to cover in the semester, and that's a lot of pressure. One of the best things you can do, sometime during those first few weeks, is to stop in before or after school and let your teacher know a little bit about yourself. For example, you may mention that you like horses.

"How about that!" Your teacher's eyes light up. "I have one of my own."

What has happened? You and the teacher have just stopped being a name on a class list and an educational talking machine. You have found something in common, and for the rest of your time together, your teacher will be more interested in you and your progress—or lack of it—just because he or she knows you a little better.

"Drop by to see the teacher? I don't think I could do it," you may say. "That's not my style!"

All right, at least begin by greeting the teacher when you walk into the classsroom. There are times when high schools must look like monasteries, simply because the students file into the room, never looking at the teacher, and never even saying, "Hi."

Students can also pass a teacher in the hall and stare right past as if the teacher were part of the woodwork. Simply acknowledging someone who is spending the better part of an hour with you five days a week is just polite and decently human. It also can be one more way for you to let that teacher know you are an individual. That's the beginning of success in the classroom.

Another reason for making yourself known to any instructor is to explain any problem you have. Telling teachers about problems you have in their class, or simply letting them know you fear some kind of failure in their subject, is not polishing the apple. It is just one way you can protect yourself from a lack of understanding, by making your teacher aware of any problems. It can do nothing but help. And sometimes just telling someone about your problems does a lot to get them into the open and under control.

There are many times when teens might need to tell their teacher of particular problems. Some, for instance, become very uncomfortable with physical education classes. Shari Cheerleader and Jim Supersport may run out on the gym floor and feel terrific. However, the girl who is very conscious of a weight problem, or of any other body feature that bothers her, may feel tense or even traumatized. The boy whose body has still not developed fully, and who has already suffered teasing in previous situations, may be going through agony when he must go out and compete with others.

Let the teacher help in these situations. If your teacher can be more sensitive to your problems, he or she can help you overcome them slowly. And the teacher can understand some of your fears and actions.

Teach the teacher about yourself. If your teacher doesn't know you, he or she will have a much harder time helping you learn. Your instructors need your help. Don't be afraid to give it.

Let the Teacher Teach   You know the teacher, at least a little bit. The teacher knows you, at least a little bit. Now what?

Now comes what your parents are paying taxes or tuition for, and what, for you, is the biggest job of your life right now. You *learn*! Or, at least you try to!

Handling each class is like handling any situation in life. Just as you read in chapter 3, the heart of education is preparing you for the future and giving you the experience you'll need to meet life head-on.

Learning in any classroom is simply adding things you don't know to things that are already a part of you. It is a building process, and although day-by-day progress may be hard to see, the structure does appear eventually.

Each class will have its own unique style, simply because each class has its own unique teacher. And even the same teacher will not teach two classes exactly the same way because of the mixture of students. One group may ask more questions, so the teacher will go along with that. Another group may be harder to handle because one or two students create discipline problems. This need for discipline will make the teacher hold to the strict lesson plan. Some classes are very quiet because students are afraid of ridicule from others. In these cases, the teacher will be more formal.

The best class you can have is one in which students feel free to ask questions. You are a part of it, and part of your job is participation. Don't be afraid to look puzzled or to raise a hand once in a while. What you don't know can be important. If you don't understand a particular concept, you can be sure someone else doesn't understand it, either. You can help others learn, as well as yourself. Sitting passively through day after day of a class only makes you bored, and it also gives the teacher the idea you don't care.

Inventory   What kind of student are you? Check what you feel applies.

___ Noncaring	___ Under pressure from parents to get good grades
___ Grade conscious	
___ Hard working	___ Bored
___ Overworked	___ Self-motivated
___ Afraid of failure	___ Pressured by class-mates not to excel
___ The ideal student	
___ A nonreader	___ No desire to succeed in school
___ No time for homework	___ Many other problems taking priority over school

Now that you've checked this list, find the negative items on it. They will be anything that keeps you from success in the classroom. You should face these problems and possibly share them with your teacher. They are your first homework. Thinking through ways to bring these problems down to size is the first step toward solving them.

Learn to Spot What Is Important

Any class will contain a lot of material. If you are really aware of the teacher, you can usually spot the information he or she is trying to stress. What the teacher repeats often he or she wants learned. What the teacher writes on the board should go in your notes. Some of the course material will simply be background and will not be essential. You must learn to spot key points. Some stores have a flashing blue or red light to call attention to special values; learn to spot the "flashing light" that signals that your teacher is hitting the hard facts.

What does the teacher review at the beginning of class? What does he or she refer back to in examples? How intense is the teacher when talking about a certain thing? What does he or she write on the board? All these are clues that will separate the meat from the fluff in any class, and they should give you a better idea of what is important.

Learning to listen also helps. Teens are absolutely great at looking directly at the teacher while their minds are as far away as the latest rock concert or that terrific little boutique in the mall. True, there will be times when your mind wanders, but try to keep it in tow most of the time. Some students get so involved watching a teacher's idiosyncrasies or noticing that he or she needs a haircut that they lose track of what the teacher is saying. Get all your noticing out of the way at the beginning of the class. Then settle down, and try to give the teacher your full attention. And as he or she speaks, don't let all those ideas that are crossing your mind distract you.

The Great Homework Conspiracy

Most classes come with an extra, added attraction—homework! Here is a word that can strike terror into the heart of any freedom-loving high schooler, but it is something we cannot pass by. A word first about the great homework conspiracy.

Any high school, usually in the morning before classes begin, will contain students sitting somewhere in the halls, on the school bus, or in an empty classroom, madly copying someone else's homework. Some students work out elaborate plans for beating the homework assignments, with each individual responsible for part of the load. At a given place, all these people converge, exchange work, and then rush off to class, thinking they have fooled the teachers and beaten the system.

Wrong! Any sane and realistic teacher knows that homework is going to get done, if it gets done, in any variety of ways. Some of it may be really worked on, studied, and learned. Other assignments will be simply copied from another's work and then handed in without any effort on the student's part.

Teachers realize this and still continue to assign homework. Why? Good instructors know that students can learn from doing the outside work and that most students will. If a student chooses to pass up a learning experience and not do the homework, that is his or her problem. The teacher also knows it will catch up with that student on the next big test.

Your mind is made for better things than finding creative ways to avoid homework. Use your intelligence for something that will be of more benefit to you, and let others who wish to, breeze along on their way toward mediocrity!

Homework hints   The secret to handling the homework problem lies in learning how to spot assignments for what they really are. Some work, such as reading, involves real learning. It is necessary for keeping up with the class, and learning to keep up in high school will make college much easier. Other assignments may be drill, and once a student knows the material, he or she can complete the work quickly and reinforce the knowledge at the same time.

Take a tip from college students. Many of them ask a teacher at the beginning of the semester to outline the class and discuss assignments, projects, and what will be expected. In this way students get an idea of what the class will be like, and then begin to plan their work schedules to handle it.

A teacher will be glad to tell you what he or she intends to cover. Your question is a chance for the teacher to show that he or she is organized and in control. Your teacher will also be happy to give you an idea of what he or she will be trying to accomplish. The teacher's job is to teach, and if he or she tells you what is planned, you will know what to expect.

Knowing what is coming will also give you time to plan for that end-of-the-semester blitz, when every teacher seems to assign long projects, and you are faced with completing them as well as studying for finals. By getting some of the work out of the way earlier, you can be sure of keeping your sanity before report card time. You can also give yourself the advantage of enjoying life while your friends are burning the candle at both ends as the semester draws to a close.

Let's get specific. How can you sensibly tackle any homework assignment? When homework is given, assess how much concentration and time are required. Then plan accordingly. Some work can be handled while you are baby-sitting. Other material will need your best shot: a quiet place and as much mental strength as you are able to muster. But do be careful that you don't reach the point where you feel you cannot concentrate without absolute silence and privacy. If you feel you can only do decent thinking under such perfect conditions, you will be setting up an unreal situation. Absolute silence and privacy are rare, so learn to tune out distractions instead of playing prima donna with the family when you are studying. The ability to concentrate even with distractions around you will be an asset for the rest of your life.

Long term projects are another matter. They require research and involve hours of outside effort. Doing papers such as these may be frightening at first, but once you learn how to plan for them and pace yourself in the time allotted, you can begin to handle them. If you plan on going to college, you are learning a valuable lesson if you can do these papers with the minimum of tension and time. You will also be far ahead of others who have never had to discipline themselves to this degree. Developing a plan of attack for long projects, with a time schedule as a guide, can help you learn to handle a large amount of work systematically.

Give yourself a break   The bottom line of education is your ability to put together new concepts and add to the material in your mental reservoir. The best teacher in the world and the most expensive computers are of no use if you do not begin to assimilate what is being presented. No one can give you learning, just as no one can give you a fine athletic body or musical ability. Learning is work—pure and simple.

Studying is not easy. It is something you must do by yourself, and it is one of the things which will take your greatest effort at this time in your life. It will also set your tone of success and ability to cope and produce throughout your life.

It is easy to ride along and squeak by on tests, to stay on the surface of the subject matter, and to promise that tomorrow you will really begin to learn. The longer you wait, however, the more you'll miss. And the less you'll have going for you when you step out into the "real world." A good way to begin studying is to set tangible goals. An *A* may be unrealistic for you, so it is good to use something other than grades as your standard. A realistic goal may be the ability to tell someone else, even if it's your kid brother, what you've learned. If you can teach it to someone else, you really know it!

Reward yourself when your goals are reached. Go ahead and give yourself a treat when you've given your best to an assignment. Let yourself feel success, and don't be afraid to be honestly proud of your achievements. Study is hard work, and if you have done it well, you deserve a break any day!

Concentration means giving your attention to one particular thing. It is never easy, but unless you develop the ability to do it during your teen years, you may never again have the opportunity to master this skill. Find a place with some semblance of peace where you will be comfortable. If music in the background helps you relax, use it. However, trying to really concentrate with the top hits blaring through your headphones is not the answer. The adult world has learned to use music as background at times, and as great entertainment at others. When you want to listen to your favorite tunes, give them the attention they deserve. When the time is set aside for study, leave the headphones off.

The amount of time you spend studying is not as important as the quality of that time. If you can give yourself to some honest work for an hour, do it. If you need a break once in a while, take it. Walk around. Watch a bit of TV. Raid the refrigerator if your conscience allows it. Then come back, put everything else on the side, and get to work again.

Give study time your best effort, set some realistic goals, and reward yourself when you are finished. You can be proud if you have tackled an assignment and done it well. And you should know that you are being fair with yourself, as well.

Someone once remarked to the author James Thurber, "You must love to write because you write so much." He surprised that person with the answer, "I hate writing.

But I love having written." That sums up the end result of study. It's never easy, but you will love having learned and accomplished the goals you set for yourself.

What you learn is not for the teacher, your folks, or your friends. The information you learn in high school will be part of you forever. If you are smart enough to take the best of what it has to offer, you're smarter than some people may think you are, and you are a richer person as well.

Rapping It Up The term "classroom" has many meanings to many people. When we talk about having class and being classy we are describing something, or someone, of high quality. It is interesting, then, that we should call that place where learning takes place a *class* room. In a way, class comes from knowing what and who you are. If education is taking place, that time you spend sitting behind a desk or computer could be time for picking up some real class.

Success in school is your challenge and your job right now. If you take the time to pick your classes wisely with an eye to the future, get to know yourself and your teachers, and give the material they present your honest best, you will succeed! You will not only be a good student, but a true winner.

If you do your best in the classroom, you certainly can become a very classy person!

Points to Ponder 1. Think back about why you chose the elective classes you did. What were your reasons?

_____

_____

_____

2. Which study method works best for you and helps you remember what you studied? Are you eye-minded, ear-minded, or action-minded?

_____

_____

_____

3. What is the hardest subject for you to learn?

   _____

   What is your main problem in studying this subject?

   _____

   _____

   Have you told your teacher about this problem?

   _____

4. Do you try to get to know your teachers and let them know you as an individual?

   _____

   If yes, how do you do it? If no, how could you do this more effectively?

   _____

   _____

   _____

Making the Grade

Society likes success. It seems everyone demands to see tangible proof that something has gone well. The successful businessperson buys a fancy car and moves to a higher class neighborhood. The superstar makes a big splash with a phenomenal wardrobe and dazzling jewelry, and the doctor hangs his or her medical diploma on the wall.

In high school there is also a way of stamping a measure of success on work. It's called—the report card!

How Did I Do? It is natural, of course, to want to know how well you have succeeded in reaching goals, and it is also natural for other people to let you know. The problem with grades comes from the great importance they carry. The actual learning of subject matter and the real mastery of certain skills can somehow fall by the roadside. If Johnny's report card is all right, Mom and Dad may be satisfied.

One of the greatest things you can do for yourself is develop a more realistic attitude toward the grades that finally show up on your report card. They are important and an indication of how well you have passed the tests, done the work, and mastered what the teacher determined as essential material.

Yet the real objective is learning, not passing. The world is full of adults who have survived high school, in the sense that they passed the classes and eventually walked out with a diploma. Many have not graduated with the mastery and knowledge they could have attained, however, and they are often unhappy with themselves because of it.

Settling for a passing grade may make your life easier now, but it also gets you into a dangerous attitude in which you are content with mediocrity. There are times all through life when one can say with satisfaction, "This will do." But if we begin to lower our standards with important things, we may dig some deep ruts that can only damage our work ethic and chances for success in years to come.

Work Ethic—What Is It?

Recently a supervisor for a top insurance company confided, "I have to fire 150 people next week. They're all under 26, and I hate to do it. But they have no commitment to the company. They put in their time, leave right at the end of the workday, and all they care about is getting a good paycheck, not about helping the company survive in these difficult times."

Sad? Yes. Why did it happen?

The answer is a concept called work ethic. It doesn't show up directly on tests, and it's very hard to pin down. It does translate into your attitude toward the work at hand, and it conveys itself to your employers and coworkers. Work ethic determines how seriously you give yourself to a project, how much motivation goes into any piece of work. It separates the winners from the also-rans. The athlete with talent doesn't always make it in the pros. If an athlete doesn't have a strong work ethic that drives him or her to stay physically in top shape, learn game plans, and always strive to win, he or she will fail.

Work ethic does not appear on report cards or in paychecks, but it can improve them. Work ethic is your own belief that hard work is a good and worthwhile thing, and a strong work ethic can lead to success in high school and later life.

Inventory   Check the statements that apply to you.

___ My pleasure is very important.	___ I am goal-oriented.
___ I need to be part of the group.	___ I can work alone.
___ I have a right to a good job.	___ I earn the things I get.
___ I have to please my folks.	___ I enjoy my own success.
___ Short-term projects are best.	___ I can see any project through.
___ I am profit motivated.	___ I am self-motivated.
___ Most work is a bore.	___ I can enjoy the product of work.
___ I'm not really a winner.	___ I believe in my ability to work.
___ I work when I have to.	___ Sometimes I enjoy work.

If you put the most checks in the left column, your work ethic is poor. Your own pleasure is still more important than your success. You have some hard growing up to do.

If you put the most checks in the right column, your work ethic is on track. Now your task is not to be better than others, but rather to improve yourself.

Where Did This Grade Come From?

That is a good question. And the answers to it are important because they help you understand the grades you will see on your next report card.

The first thing to understand is that each class has a rating and evaluation system of its own. Math and English are both basic courses and may even be taught in a similar way. They are very different, though, and your understanding of each will be measured in different ways.

Some classes are very regimented, and the material is precise. Math does not leave much room for interpretation. The figures are there. The process is there. If you keep the figures and process right, you come up with the one and only right answer.

Reading a short story for English is a different ball game. The author had his or her own reason for writing the story, the teacher has his or her own interpretation, and you may have your own valid ideas on the story. No one is wrong. When an audience reads a story, they read from their own experience and may get some ideas the author never considered. Many people read symbolism into writing which was never really intended. Words are a catalyst for thought. Any thinker, then, will read different things into a story. Interpretation is a subjective activity, although you should always try to support your theories with facts from the story.

Let's be objective

When your teacher gives you a math grade, it comes from a series of test scores and homework assignments. How many problems did you get right? How much work did you accomplish? In a math class, the grading system is simple and always objective. Whether you smile at the teacher, spend hours studying, or breeze through it because it is easy, somehow gets lost. The grade itself simply shows how many answers you got right or wrong.

Any class in which your grade is determined in an objective manner is one in which you can keep track of progress with the teacher. By keeping your test scores, you can know what your average is, and you can do something about it before the grading period ends.

This subject is too subjective!

In other classes, where the grading is more subjective, your progress can be harder to assess. How well you complete a project in shop or a home economics class is something the teacher determines. The grade does not come from being right or wrong, but from meeting a defined set of standards that the teacher uses to evaluate material.

When you hand in an English composition, there may be points off for misspelling or grammatical errors. Even though English teachers often use two grades—one for content and one for technical skills—the grade tends to be subjective. In classes such as these, is wise to talk to the teacher from time to time and ask what he or she expects from a project. If you can understand the teacher's standards, you have a better chance of meeting them when grade time nears.

Too many students go blindly ahead on projects, do what *they* feel is right, and then hand them in. When they get the grade, they complain, then develop negative and bitter feelings. Once that grade is given, though, it is too late. Knowing *beforehand* is the only way to set your own standards and understand what is expected of you.

One thing you will want to check is that your grade comes only from your academic progress. A good reporting system may include grades given for conduct and effort, but they should be separate from academic grades.

If you have a tendency to talk a lot in class, or for some reason make the teacher feel you are a discipline problem, this should not be reflected in your academic grade. You may get an *A* in the subject and an *F* in conduct, but these grades should be separate. If you feel there is some problem in this area, a good talk with the teacher should set things straight.

Changing Grades

Contrary to public opinion, teachers do not wear bullet-proof vests on report card day. True, they dread it as much as students, but what they really dislike is knowing some students will invariably come after report cards have been handed out, asking or demanding that their grade be changed.

The time for worrying about grades is during the grading period. Once that time is over and a teacher has come up with averages and grades, he or she is not terribly excited about being challenged on a particular mark. Don't let yourself become one of the angry horde that moves from classroom to classroom after school on report card day, arguing and pleading with teachers to change grades.

However, if you feel a grade is unjust or a mistake has been made, you have every right to approach a teacher. Just be prepared to do so in a reasonable manner. Carrying on and moaning that you will be grounded or lose your car privileges is not a mature or acceptable way of behaving. It only lowers the teacher's opinion of you and marks you as a whiner who has probably gotten by for years with similar tactics. It also does nothing for your own self-esteem, and if classmates are around when you go into your routine, they may not have much respect for you, either!

Safe at Home?

Report cards are meant for your parents as well as for you. The school wants to communicate your progress to the home front, and so far the best way to do that is by using report cards. This is especially necessary in high school, when most parents do not bother to meet or communicate on a regular basis with their children's teachers.

One way you can soften the blow of report cards is to encourage your parents to meet teachers during open house, or talk periodically with them on the phone. Personal communication is much more satisfactory than a cold grade plunked on a computer printed report card. It will also give both your folks and your teachers a better understanding of each other, as well as you.

Some parents, sad to say, put unreal pressure on their children. If Dad was a Rhodes Scholar, and all your older brothers and sisters came home with straight A's, you may be under the gun to bring home nothing less. If you feel your parents expect more than you can honestly deliver, an attempt at communication will go a long way. Your parents want you to be a success, and they want you to be the best. That's normal. If you feel they don't understand some of your problems in a particular class, however, it is up to you to get that message across in a calm, not whiny, way.

Unfair Grades   You may also run into a class where a teacher is a hard grader, and an A is hard to come by. You may meet a male teacher who feels it is impossible for a girl to get an *A* in driver's ed, or you may find a teacher who thinks a master computer would have difficulty pulling a top grade in her calculus class. Such teachers are rare, but they do still exist. If you happen to get them for a class during your school career, you may have to learn another lesson this early in life. If you feel the teacher is simply difficult, letting your parents know about the situation will help make the report card go down a bit easier. If, however, you feel you are the victim of real discrimination—be it because of your sex, color, or any other minority status—you do have avenues for seeking help. First of all, follow the chain of command. This is the proper way to handle any problem—now and in the future.

The first person you address is the teacher. Express your concerns, and ask for some straight answers. If the situation still does not change, your next step is the department head. Is an English teacher your problem? Ask for a meeting with the English department head, and express your concerns. If no help is given, go to the principal. State and federal laws are very definite on discrimination, and your principal is very aware of them. He or she should take care of the matter. If not, there is always the superintendent of schools and members of the school board.

You may be young, but you do have the right to fair and unbiased treatment. Don't be afraid to claim that right.

Reading a Report Card

Report cards are for you, too. If you just take them and slip them into your pocket until that fateful moment at home, you're missing something you can do for yourself.

First, a report card is one way to find out what someone else thinks of your performance. Grades do come from what you do and fail to do in class. They also give teachers a chance to assess your progress. All through your life, others will be judging your work, and if you can learn to honestly stare down that report card and accept what it says, you are one more step up on the ladder of maturity.

Don't, in any case, compare your card with a classmate's. Report card time is not a contest; it's a special time for you and your teacher to share an evaluation of what you have done. Pitting yourself against others only makes you feel bad if you score below them, or feel wrongfully superior if you have higher grades. Your grade is for *you*, and that's where it should stop.

Get some help

One good practice is to talk to your teacher or counselor after a grading period. These people are working with you, and they know your potential. Let them help you decide what is a good grade in each particular subject. In this way you can learn to set realistic goals. By talking with people who know you and know what standards you are up against, you can get a good estimate of your own ability and save yourself a lot of tension and sorrow.

Another practice that might help is to make out your own report card a day or two before grades are issued. Being honest with yourself, put down grades for each of your classes, then assess them against what you feel you could be doing. If you are satisfied with the comparison, you know you are giving your best effort.

Rapping It Up

No one likes to be judged. No one likes to be told he or she is not good at something. Report cards, if you let them, can become prophets of doom. But they can also become valuable tools to help you sort out your own successes and accomplishments. They can give you an objective look at how you are mastering the skills that high school demands, and how you are living up to the standards and goals you have set for yourself.

Fearing report cards is foolish. Any coach who loses a game tries to understand why. He or she is honest and tries to see where things could have been better. The coach then makes the corrections as best as possible, and comes out fresh for the next game. If a coach dwelt on past failures, he or she would never have the courage to go out and try again.

You, too, can learn to make report cards work for you and guide you to a more successful high school experience. Let report cards be a tool, not a torment. Use them well, and then move on to the next grading period. You are getting older. Also, you are getting wiser, and with a little honest effort on your part, you will certainly get better, too.

Points to Ponder

1. Do you get your biggest pressure for grades from your parents or yourself?

   _____

2. Are grades becoming more important or less important to you?

   _____

   Why? _____

   _____

   _____

3. Are you achieving at what are realistically high standards for you?

   _____

4. How can you use your report card to help understand your own success or lack of it?

   _____

   _____

   _____

5. Grade your work ethic: _____. Now write a brief essay

on how your attitude and approach to work and projects
could be improved. List specific things you could do to
improve the quality of your schoolwork and get better
grades.

_____

_____

_____

_____

_____

_____

_____

_____

_____

_____

_____

_____

Teachers and Administrators

That old joke, "It's not the school, it's the principal of the thing!" still gets a laugh, but many teens see no humor in the presence of the teachers and administrators in their schools. Teachers have always been the object of jokes and scathing humor. They stand in front of the classroom as the adults in charge; they make the decisions, and some of them have earned the true dislike of their students. Teachers, however, are also human, and some of them can claim partial responsibility for the success and the really productive lives of thousands of students.

Teens are young people on the move. They are on the way up, and as they begin to find more independence within and outside of the home, they are justified in their attempts to prove themselves. In school, however, something happens. Just when parents have begun to allow more freedom, a new set of authority figures comes in and takes over. Teachers and counselors, hall monitors, the principal and assistant principals appear on the scene and are armed with rules, regulations, and guidelines for discipline. No wonder teens, especially if they have trouble coping with authority figures in their lives, soon develop a negative attitude toward adults within the school.

Not All Teachers Are Terrific

Before you decide how you feel about teachers, it's best not to think of them as a group. Of course, you and everyone else can tell stories about bad teachers who ridicule their students in front of the class, who make unreasonable assignments and demands, and who may have caused serious psychological harm to the young people who are entrusted to their care. These, fortunately, are a small minority of teachers. They have gotten mixed up somewhere along the way. They have problems and certainly should not be part of any school system. If you run across these teachers, recognize the problem, try not to let their bitterness spread to you, and, if you are a strong enough person, try to forgive them for their ignorance.

Any teacher who is a problem to others is in exactly the same position as a problem student. It is not normal to be bitter, cynical, or to lack respect for others. When people possess these characteristics, no matter at what age, they have a problem in their own personality. They need help and guidance, and until they can get straightened out, they need understanding and sympathy.

Some teachers cannot tolerate their opinion being challenged. They view open discussion as a threat to their authority, and you will have to tolerate this attitude during class. The biggest lesson these instructors can teach you is a very important one—don't imitate them!

Are There Any Good Teachers?

Once you can get beyond your own hang-ups about authority, you may begin to realize that many teachers have a lot to offer. A good teacher can spur you on to new interests. He or she can challenge you to reach down and find talent and ability inside yourself that you never knew existed. A good teacher can also become a guide, and even a friend, who understands and really wishes the best for you.

The teacher who tries to see you as an individual and who is aware of your needs and problems can help in many ways. He or she may sometimes give you help or advice on matters that go beyond the classroom. For example, a good teacher will certainly be able to help you when you start looking for your first good job and can make you aware of some of the successes in your life that you tend to overlook.

Student Attitude versus Teacher Attitude

One of the experiences taking place millions of times each day in our country is the confrontation of student attitude against teacher attitude. If you, as a student, walk into class with a chip on your shoulder, expecting the worst, you will transmit that feeling to the teacher. And you may get the worst!

If, on the other hand, you enter each class presuming real learning and sharing can take place, most teachers will respond to that feeling and try to do their best for you.

Just as your mother may get upset and never feel like cooking again if no one eats her gourmet meal, a teacher needs some stimulation and interest from the class to keep producing his or her best. If a teacher feels no one is interested, and boredom is beginning to set in, that teacher may lose enthusiasm too and let the class become a boring routine.

Turn back to chapter 4 and find the positive, open attitude you buried—the mind-set where you expect the best from yourself and others. Dust it off, and take it into the classroom. You may see a change in the attitude of your teacher, as well.

Make Them Teach

You should expect good, honest teaching when you walk into a classroom. Teachers tend to fall into a routine and may simply present the material as they have in the past. If a topic is glossed over too lightly, and you still don't feel you understand it, raise your hand. Ask for more information. Give the teacher a chance to discuss the matter more thoroughly. Make the teacher tell you all he or she knows. You may get a lot more than you bargained for, and after a few classes like this, you may discover your teacher is coming to class a bit more prepared, with more than just surface information.

Another way you can help yourself and the teacher is in asking him or her to relate the subject matter to your current life. A good teacher should really be a master of the material. However, sometimes a teacher may be too intent on covering facts and may forget to take time to respond to the immediate interests you may have.

If you think a class is becoming dull, try to ask some questions that can bring in current events. Help the teacher bring the outside world into the classroom and the lectures. Good teachers can cover the material *and* keep the class interesting. By bringing new material to the course, you may give your teacher a new lease on teaching. And you'll have one less boring class to worry about!

Take Time to Communicate

One of the key things to remember about your experience in school is that you're dealing with people. Some of the most important people you meet during the day are your teachers.

Communication is the key. Giving teachers a glimpse into your world and what is important to you will encourage them to be human, too. It will give your teachers that extra motivation to do their best for you. When people are working together, the personal communication that flows between them often makes the difference between mediocrity and excellence.

A ball game on a rainy, cold day, with no crowd in the stands, can be boring. Even the players lose that special spark. There is no one to respond, to give that extra drive. As a result, the game loses all electricity. And a class in which the students sit dully in their seats, barely listening, never questioning, and never taking time to respond or show any interest can make the teacher react the same way. The lights may still be on, but there is no spark of electricity in the class.

Do you want good teachers? Then you—yes, *you*—can help make them good teachers.

Do you want your classes to be more interesting and exciting? You are the key to the problem. If you let your teachers know you want their best, not only will they produce for you, but they'll also begin to respect you more. They will be more understanding of your needs and more open to your opinions.

The Principal—The Most Misunderstood Boss

The principal! There he or she is—innocently walking down the hall. As the principal passes, you may wonder where the ax is about to fall.

Possibly the most feared and misunderstood person in any school is the principal. The principal is at a disadvantage because he or she cannot get to know students the way teachers can. The principal can't meet with the same individuals every day, but he or she is expected to handle countless problems, be a friend and counselor to all the students, and keep the whole school running on an even keel. The principal's job is difficult!

You may say, "So what? Why should I care?" Well, the principal is in a position of authority; he or she can be a big help to you. The principal can toss you out of school or make life better for you. If the principal knows you, he or she can help you with references and good advice when you choose a college or set out to find a serious job. You can be sure that many businesspeople know your principal. They will probably be more than willing to listen when he or she speaks. So if you can get the principal to speak well about you, you'll have a great advantage.

Try to make yourself known to the principal in some positive way during the year. A smile and a "hi" will usually be all it takes. Most principals see the small percentage of students who get into trouble. They are eager to meet the rest of the student body. Most principals have a teaching background, and they often miss the personal contact with students that teachers enjoy every day. By offering a friendly smile, or finding some way for the principal to become aware of you, you can do the principal and yourself a favor.

Help Your Own Cause

By learning to be friendly with teachers and administrators, you can make your years in school happier and more successful. You will also give yourself some practice dealing with authority figures. Then when you are in the adult work world, you will have an advantage over other employees who feared and mistrusted authority during their school years, and continue to do so.

Those in positions higher than yours are not necessarily tyrannical, mean, or awesome. They are simply people doing a job. And when authority figures can feel the support and positive attitudes of others, they tend to be more human and understanding themselves.

The fear and lack of trust many adults have for everyone from police officers to politicians did not happen overnight. Many people who carry these feelings began by fearing and mistrusting their teachers and principals. They may have had domineering parents or been abused by people who used their power in wrong ways. Whatever their reason, those who fear authority are at a great disadvantage in life.

Rapping It Up   If you can learn to deal in a positive way with the people who have authority in your life, your relationships with bosses and teachers are sure to be better. You may also learn to retain your own humanity and willingness to understand when you are placed in a position of authority yourself.

Teachers and administrators are human. They will have their up and down days. They have moods, successes, and lapses of genius just as you do. You as a student are probably very conscious of your own individuality. You want people to respond to it. You want them to be fair and to try to understand your personal needs. You want some plain human respect! Your teachers are in the same situation. Most of them are conscious of their responsibility to prepare you for the world, and most want to give you the best they can offer.

The few who are poor teachers or difficult personalities are probably out of touch with the important things in life. You will find people like them everywhere, and you must learn how to deal with them. By accepting their shortcomings and trying to understand these teachers, you can make yourself a more tolerant and humane person. You can also develop the strong advantage of being able to deal with all kinds of people, even the difficult ones.

The next time you are baby-sitting, or find yourself in some circumstance where you possess authority, take a minute to realize what is happening. How are you handling the power? You will realize that authority carries as much responsibility as it does prestige. The one who wields power has to try extra hard to be patient, understanding, and tolerant of others.

Most teachers know those feelings and are trying to do their best. By giving teachers your respect and consideration, you can help them accomplish their job. With your help, teachers and administrators can give you the best of their knowledge and the best of their personalities. And, they can help you become your very best!

Points to Ponder   1. Name four characteristics of a good teacher.

_____

_____

_____

_____

2. How can you help your teachers have better classes?

    _____

    _____

    _____

3. What qualities do you dislike in teachers?

    _____

    _____

    Have you ever shown the same characteristics?

    _____

    _____

    What would help you get along better with teachers you dislike?

    _____

    _____

4. What is your attitude toward the principal and his or her assistants?

    _____

    _____

    Is it based on fear or real knowledge? _____

    Explain. _____

    _____

5. Would you be a good teacher or principal? _____ Why?

    _____

    _____

    _____

Beyond the Classroom

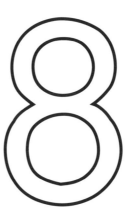

Many high school graduates agree on one thing. They may have learned a good deal about traditional subjects, but of the many things they remember, most were events never reflected on a report card. Any student who walks away from high school without participating in extracurricular activities, without sitting in the stands and cheering for the home team, has passed up some of the happiest times and opportunities for growth he or she may see for some time. It is a great mistake to think of school only as a place to put in class time and get out as quickly as possible.

As your teen years roll by, you are growing and developing. Involvement in school activities can open new avenues of interest for you and help you develop a lot of characteristics that will be expected of you as an adult. Some of the most important aspects of adult life are knowing how to give, how to accept responsibility, and how to develop and retain a sense of loyalty. As a child, you have often been on the receiving end. People give you much when you are young, but it is dangerous for you to feel that life will always be that way.

Guess what? It is not front page news, of course, but the older you get, the more others will expect of you. Involvement in school activities can make it easier for you to meet those expectations.

People Skills

One class that never appears in your schedule is "People 101." The social studies, math, English, and science classes are there, but where is the slot in your schedule for learning to relate to others?

Once there was a student who walked away from every grading period with A's. The teachers and principal praised him, and all seemed to be well. But this student, with all his knowledge and good intentions, was slipping through high school without learning to deal with people. He was nice to them, but never seemed to understand them well. As a result, this student soon became an object of ridicule when he was out of hearing range.

Teachers couldn't understand it. The principal thought other students were simply jealous. But the other students themselves realized the problem. This student was simply "out of it." He was learning all the book knowledge, but he wasn't learning the simple art of common sense. He could understand textbooks, but couldn't respond in a common, ordinary way to people.

This young man is in college now. With some luck, he is learning to relate better to those around him. He may be a success with books, but unless he begins to learn the simple lesson of understanding others, he will have disastrous relationships with his co-workers and anyone else who tries to become part of his life.

Get Involved

The simple fact is that books can't teach you everything. What is the best way to learn to deal with people?

If you learn to really watch the people you meet and observe their reactions, that can be a good start. Another way to improve your social skills is to get involved with outside-the-classroom activities at your school.

Do you like to write, or see your work actually find its way to print? Get on the school paper or yearbook staff. Do you like to work with your hands? Join an art or car club.

How about sports? Terrific! If you can't make the varsity team, there is always the neighborhood sandlot game, intramurals, and the self-satisfaction of competing, trying, and sometimes winning.

Whatever you choose, your school provides dozens of opportunities to get involved with people. Extracurricular groups also provide you with projects that do not directly involve book learning, but that can help you tremendously. By working with others and facing the demands of situations, you can begin to develop your skill for dealing with people. In this way, common sense and the ability to read people will become part of your life.

Share the load

Extracurricular activities are a good way of meeting people who have similar interests and potential. These activities also offer a more realistic climate than the classroom. Pressure may be there, but it is usually shared. The need for success in a play, game, or club project is shared by the entire group. In the classroom, you succeed or fail on your own effort at strict, academic knowledge. In a club or activity, you share the load with others who want success, and you'll be working for goals that are meaningful to all of you. That is also a way to make the kind of friends who last—the kind who share your same interests and likes.

Build some good memories

There may be an adult or two who says, "Enjoy your high school years. They're the happiest time of your life." That statement is sad, in a way, because if a person is really to develop the maximum potential for feeling, loving, succeeding, and being fulfilled, high school will not be the greatest-all-time years of life. As an adult, a person should be able to live a deeper and richer existence and find a fuller kind of happiness than is possible for teens.

You can take many good memories during your high school years, however. That may be what some of those adults are remembering—in addition to the fact that they didn't have to pay all the bills and shoulder all the responsibilities they have now. The times when you laugh and "go bananas" because of unbelievably happy situations, and times when you feel that quiet, confident sense of success and satisfaction inside yourself—these are some of the happiest and most rewarding times of life! Involvement in extracurricular activities can provide the opportunity for some of these times.

The academic subjects are important, even if this doesn't seem so now. Besides the knowledge you are getting, they give you the discipline to organize your mind and expand your ideas. Academic courses are essential, but they cannot give you a complete education and thrust into the future by themselves. Where they leave off, extracurricular activities should take over.

By screaming your lungs out at a game, meeting the pressure of yearbook deadlines, perfecting a special piece of music for a concert, or working through the excitement of a play, you can help educate yourself. These activities also will be the ones you remember when your own children are in school. They may also be your fondest memories of high school.

Yes, those adults who tell you high school was the happiest time are probably remembering the thrill of taking a bow at the spring play, or the pleasure they felt when their pet idea made it through the student council.

It's Not All Pom-Poms and Praise

Of course getting involved in other activities at school does not ensure perpetual happiness and constant success. Working with other people naturally means you are rubbing elbows with many different types, and there may be someone who challenges your ideas and seems to thwart everything you want to do.

There also may be times when the goal you work hard for is not achieved. You may spend hours doing a mural for a school hallway only to have someone come by and make fun of it. The story in the school paper you took three nights to complete may end up in the trash can, and, after all your effort, you still might lose the big game.

"That's exactly right," you say. "So why bother getting involved? Who needs the grief?"

You do, friend, because it's not just grief. It's learning. And that's life. Do you want to feel you are becoming an adult? Do you want to be able to walk into a room and feel you've added something besides extra weight? Part of learning common sense and deepening yourself as a person comes from facing the difficult experiences as well as the easy. By involving yourself in something that takes the best you have to offer, you can learn what it is to really try and to really give.

And the setbacks and hard times only make your final success sweeter.

Rapping It Up

So, there you sit, wondering what to do. "Life is dull," you say. "Everything is such a bore! There's nothing to do in this town." Maybe you're right. You may live in the deadest town in the world, one where little entertainment is available. However, there is a solution!

You can make your own entertainment by getting into the action. You can get over your boredom by joining others who are involved in life, not letting it pass them by.

Hobbies and interests can make the difference. One way to find out what you really enjoy is to explore the possibilities that exist within your own school. By geting involved, you may even start seeing some possible career opportunities. You will also learn how to deal with people in real-life situations. You'll learn how to be a good team player, and even a good leader. You'll learn how to cope with pressure and how to share, and you may find that your greatest source of happiness and fulfillment lies within yourself.

You wouldn't go on a long trip without taking all the things you think you will need. Don't give less thought to your life. It takes everything you can give to prepare for that adult life up ahead. And if you want to learn it all, it isn't just in the books. It's also in the people. Get out where the people are and you'll walk out of high school with a real education.

Points to Ponder

1. What keeps you from getting more involved in school activities?

   _____

   _____

2. What was the last school function you attended?

   _____

   Did you enjoy it? _____

3. How did you meet the friends you now have?

   _____

   _____

What kind of new friends would you like to meet and why?

_____

_____

4. What do you do to fight off feelings of boredom when they hit?

_____

_____

5. What extracurricular activities are available at your school? Which ones appeal to you?

_____

_____

Don't Stagnate— Communicate!

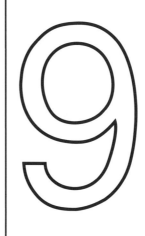

"Now, here's one chapter I can skip," you say. "If there's one thing I can really do well, it's talk!"

Before you decide, though, take a second and ask yourself if you're really able to say all you want to when you talk to others. Are you satisfied with the level of communication you have with your friends? Do you let the adults in your life know what's on your mind in other ways than merely complaining or arguing? In short, are you communicating what is inside of you to the people who matter in your life?

Communication, of course, is more than words. On all its different levels, it includes body language, use of speech, and the high art form of listening. The ability to share our deepest feelings and thoughts make humans superior to other life forms, some feel. It gives us a special edge in making life richer and more rewarding. Since we are not hermits, communication is one of our greatest tools.

No One Understands Me!

You, and everyone else on this planet, want to be understood. You know you're a unique person, and you want others to realize that and respond to your individuality. There are ways of asserting your feelings and making your opinions known, but sometimes teens latch on to the wrong ones.

Vandalism, for example, communicates a lack of respect and mistrust of society. The teen who rips up school or public property is shouting loudly and clearly that he or she has no use for what society values. In the same way, a teen who steals merchandise at a local store is sending the world a message—that he or she has found a way to beat the system.

These actions may stem from a deeper problem in these individuals. Perhaps they have not learned how to communicate their frustrations and ideas, so they vent their tensions in unacceptable ways. Like the loudmouth in class, their need to be boisterous or antagonizing comes from insecurity.

One of the greatest problems people of all ages face is the inability to get through to others. Teens, especially, often feel they must learn to make it alone, and, as a result, they keep too much on the inside. That's a mistake. If you want people to understand you, you must first let them know you. Your physical appearance and the way you conduct yourself may give others some hints about who you are, but not until you open up and make an honest effort at communication can they really begin to respond.

Open Up

One of the biggest complaints from adults is "Teens don't talk!" True, some of your teachers may feel you have no difficulties in this regard, but many adults feel they cannot communicate with young people.

Many teens, when faced with new situations, tend to drift off to the silent sidelines. Monosyllabic answers or a series of grunts are all they seem to manage, and as a result many people give up trying to get through to them.

Shyness or lack of confidence can create some lack of communication skills. However, a simple cure lies in recognizing the successes you've had in the past. As a teen you may feel people are passing judgement on you, but they really are not. The give and take of normal life does not allow for time to judge and make major decisions about everyone we meet. Most people just want to find out who you are and what you're all about. If you can relax and help by talking to them, the rest comes naturally.

You Figure It Out

Identify possible solutions in each of these cases involving communication problems:

1. Brian doesn't get the after-school job he wants because the store owner says Brian doesn't speak up loudly enough to deal with people.

   _____

   _____

2. Debbie is accused of being sneaky and possibly dishonest because she doesn't look people in the eye when talking with them.

   _____

   _____

3. Cindy won't go out with Mark because she feels he can't carry on a decent conversation with her or any of her friends.

   _____

   _____

Develop Humility and Self-Respect

The ability to communicate presumes a few things of any individual. First, you must have a certain amount of humility and respect for others' opinions. To achieve honest communication with someone, you must want to share with that person and know what he or she is thinking. You have to care about him or her as a person.

The supreme egotist, who walks into a room and waits for everyone's head to turn, is too self-absorbed to really care what anyone else thinks. He or she has never realized that communication is a two-way street. Instead, the egotist believes that if you want to listen, fine; if not, others are just dying to hear the pearls of wisdom.

If you can bring yourself to care about others, and try to develop an honest interest in what they have to offer, you will transmit this feeling to them. And they'll be more than happy to want to speak with you.

Honest communication also demands a healthy respect for yourself.

"That's a laugh," you say. "I spend half my life trying to fight off put-downs, and you tell me to respect myself!"

Absolutely. It is true that by the time you reach your teens you may have been thoroughly bombarded by instructions from adults and peers to keep quiet about your accomplishments. They have told you to be humble and think little of yourself. But what is true humility?

Let's go back to the idea of the egotist. Egotists have no problem respecting their own warped opinion of themselves, but that isn't what true humility, or lack of it, is all about. Truly humble people can honestly accept what they are and what they are not. If you're a good musician, it would be foolish to say you are not. By acknowledging that fact and living comfortably with it, you are humble. Humility is simply accepting the truth about yourself, both good and bad. If you can do that, you can learn to develop honest and realistic respect for yourself.

That self-respect will be your hidden advantage when you try to share with others. It will also be a major key to your success.

Learn to Really Look

The next time you're talking with someone, take the time to sit back and really look that person in the eyes. Is the person looking at you? Do his or her eyes show that special spark of interest, or do they keep wandering off?

Does the person seem nervous or relaxed and at ease? Notice body language. A good book on body language may be worthwhile if you would like to understand more about what people are saying to you while you are with them. By understanding body language, you can learn to be more subtle in your approach to people and respond better to their mood or disposition at that time.

Listen with Intelligence

Nodding your head occasionally is a way of letting people feel you are listening during a conversation, but sometimes it can backfire. If you want to carry on a conversation with someone, don't be afraid to ask questions, ask for more information on a topic, and even disagree at times. If a person mentions something he or she presumes you know, and you don't know it, don't be afraid to say so.

"It looked like a Henway to me," someone might say.

You have no idea what a Henway is. However, rather than show your possible ignorance, you nod and flash your all-knowing look of unquestionable wisdom. Pretending you know what you don't know certainly can backfire, as it would in this case. If you had enough self-assurance to ask what a Henway was, your conversation would have gone like this:

"What's a Henway?"

"About five pounds!"

A trick? A joke? Maybe. But it's also a little way to catch a person playing super all-knowing genius when in reality he or she certainly is not! Ignorance is all right. It means you simply haven't had a chance to learn something. Stupidity, of course, is another matter. Stupidity is thinking or pretending that you know everything!

Talk with People

Another way to sharpen your communication skills is to talk *with* people instead of *at* them. A good speaker is always aware of the audience. He or she knows them, and knows how to speak to them in a way they will find comfortable.

Real communication involves being open to others' opinions and interests. If you find you have little to say, you may not know the other person well enough. Slowly building up knowledge of others can give you some basic information, and once you find a common ground, you should be able to launch some fairly good conversations.

Caring about others and what is important to them is the key to better communication. Once you can master this, you'll be at ease in any conversation. Others, sensing your interest, will respond in a favorable, friendly way to you.

Talking down to people, on the other hand, is a sure-fire way of cutting off real communication, and it is only the approach of the egotist.

Don't interrupt

One common criticism of young people is that they cannot listen to more than two sentences without interrupting. This is especially true if the other person is voicing an opinion that goes against the teen's thought. Whether it's a parent trying to make a point, a teacher trying to explain why your work is not satisfactory, or a friend simply disagreeing with your point of view, your approach should be the same: Let the person talk, and don't interrupt.

Listening accomplishes two things. It lets the speaker feel he or she has gotten an opinion across to you. It also makes the speaker feel there can be good communication, because by listening you have shown that you understand what good communication is all about.

Listening also helps you. By listening to all someone has to say to you, you can understand the other person's point of view. Even if you disagree, listening helps you analyze the person's logic and form your response. By constantly interrupting when your opinion is under assault, you simply help communication break down. The other person feels you are hostile, and you are so busy defending yourself that you cannot come up with a logical, acceptable answer to any of the things he or she is saying.

Meet on Common Ground

Much is written about the communication gap between teens and adults. Parents and teens often feel they are on two different wavelengths. Some teens even prefer it that way. Your boss may be a middle-aged man or woman who seems impossible to talk to, and he or she, in turn, may think there is no way to get through to you.

Sometimes even your friends seem on a different planet; something comes between you. Their interests are going off in other directions, and you just can't seem to talk with them anymore.

In order for real communication to take place, both people must be able to relax and meet on common ground. Playing games with people, and fearing to be honest with them, is a form of insincerity. When communication seems most difficult, that's when you must try the hardest to understand the other person's concerns. No communication can take place in the home, for example, if both parents and teens refuse to acknowledge each other's position. But, if parent and child can sit down and share a common concern with respect for each other's opinions, real communication can occur.

Sincere communication has no room for rivalry, dishonesty, or feelings of superiority. The basic core of good relationships with people is the ability to share. If two people think they have a relationship when, in fact, they cannot be honest and share their feelings with each other, they are living a sham.

Be Yourself

Consider this situation. Debbie wants to date Jack, and when he finally asks her out, all she cares about is that Jack will like her. As a result, Deb puts on a show. She immediately agrees with everything Jack mentions, and when he suggests she get involved with the ski club, she meekly agrees. Months of agony on the slopes may be ahead for Debbie; she hates snow and considers her time outside during winter simply as basic human survival until spring.

Wanting a relationship is normal. Going against your own feelings and what is important to you, though, is a way of selling yourself out for a little popularity or security. If Debbie could be honest with Jack and admit that she would really like to see him more often, and that there must be other things they might share, Jack might realize he has finally met an honest girl with whom he can also be honest.

If Jack has the attitude, "Love me, love my skis," then Debbie is better off knowing that at the beginning of the relationship. She can decide if Jack is worth it, and if she really does not care to become a snow bunny, she can begin to look elsewhere for someone else.

Relationships that begin on dishonest terms may seem terrific for a while. If the games never stop, however, only heartache and frustration can result. Save yourself a lot of grief, and be yourself.

Words Are Worth It

Have you ever caught yourself sitting in a parking space, waiting to turn off the car because you want to hear the end of a special song? Join the club. The best songs, the very special ones, are those that capture a feeling, a thought, or a memory very dear to us. They touch the center of our being, or they give us special joy. Why? Because they say what is deepest and most important to us. They remind us of something beautiful. These are the special songs we have shared with someone we love.

The words make these songs great. Someone, somewhere, feeling the same sensation and daring to risk failure, spent the energy and effort to write these feelings down and try to share them with others.

Communication can come in the form of words like "Take out the garbage" and "Clean your bedroom." But communication reaches its peak in special words like "I love you" and "I understand."

Let your feelings flow

Stripping away some of your protective shield and actually letting others see the "real you" is risky. You risk the possibility of rejection and misunderstanding. You risk being hurt. Using words, however, is the only way others can understand what we have to offer. And when the people who reject us, or don't understand us, walk away, the ones who are left can become our dearest friends and our greatest aides in life.

The only people who are never criticized or rejected are those who never do anything. They stay safe and secure behind their self-erected walls and seem to be very comfortable. But they will never know the joy of true friendship or the thrill of sharing the beautiful things of life with another person who really understands.

You have the choice—to share your true self with others or to remain isolated. You are the only one who can activate that part of your success. Will you survive high school? If you can break down the barriers you or other people have built, and initiate some honest communication, you can do more than survive your teen years. You can ensure a lifetime of personal satisfaction and beautiful relationships.

Rapping It Up   Your life will be as successful as your communication skills allow it to be. In our society, with pressures and problems confronting everyone, it is necessary to share some of them with others. In our age of computers, people are desperately searching for other people who can remind them of what plain, simple, human living is all about. And the more image and stereotype begin to invade the television programming and magazine pages, the harder it becomes to be yourself and be honest with others.

You, with youth on your side, can begin to turn things around for yourself and the rest of the world. You can begin to knock down some of those images and start communicating on human levels. People need each other. They need to be able to get their feelings and opinions across to others.

Start slowly. A smile, a nod, a friendly "hello" will let others know you are not afraid to strike up a casual relationship. Meeting people is half the battle. Once they know you, liking you should be rather easy.

Don't be afraid to talk to adults. They have only two advantages over you. Some of them may be bigger, and all of them have had more experience. These two things aside, they are simply people who are trying to live their lives as fully as they can, just as you are. In fact, many adults genuinely fear you, thinking you are smarter than they are or that you will reject them because they are "out of it." By letting them know you are willing to meet them on equal terms and share what you have in common, you can establish the basis for exciting communication, and also become a more mature person.

Grunts and arguments can get some thoughts across. Real words honestly spoken, however, work much better. Try using them!

Points to Ponder

1. How well do your good friends really understand you?

   _____

   _____

2. What do you feel people don't understand about you, and why?

   _____

   _____

3. How would you rate your ability to participate in a class discussion?

   _____

   How can it improve? _____

4. When do you feel least shy? _____

   Why are you more comfortable in some situations than others?

   _____

   _____

5. Do you feel you can communicate with adults?

   _____

   What would make communicating with them easier?

   _____

   _____

Riding toward the Future with Your Friends

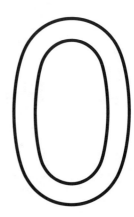

The basketball team has just lost the sectional championship in the last few seconds of the game. The cheering section sits, stunned. Parents filter slowly from the stands, trying not to watch the winning team cut down the nets.

In the locker room Mike sits alone. His hair is drenched with perspiration, and his eyes are wet with stinging tears. The agonizing silence seems to keep drumming, "We lost!"

Suddenly a tall shadow falls across the emptiness of that dim locker room. It's Jim, Mike's best friend and teammate, the one who was always there with a joke. Jim reaches out and for a moment touches Mike's shoulders to let Mike know it's okay. This hard time, with two good friends sharing it, is still difficult, but it is also a special time.

Friendship is a very precious thing. Your friends are some of the most important people in your life, and if you can enjoy the special things with them, you are fortunate.

Friends make life easier, and they are some of your valuable allies as you attempt to make the most of this thing called high school. Your friends are very much like you and, besides having the ability to persuade you to act like them, they can share in your priorities and goals.

Choosing Wisely

"Choose, nothing! I'll take all the friends I can get!" you may say. But do choose wisely. Be aware that when someone becomes your friend, you begin to accept many of that person's likes and dislikes. The attitudes and values of your friends will influence the way you think and evaluate things for many years to come.

Some teens, feeling lonely and left out, make concessions. They are willing to become friends with almost anyone just to make sure they won't be forced to spend night after night at home with their kid brothers and sisters watching reruns on television.

Others, feeling popularity will make them the envy of their classmates, get involved with large groups of people, commonly called cliques. Whatever the reason, many young people, fearing they may miss the best times of their teens, make friends too easily. Only later do they face some decisions about their choices.

The circle of friendship

A common mistake is wanting too many people to be friends with you. Looking at a clique, or even at the varsity football team, you may get the false idea that others have more friends than you. True, these students may have more people acknowledge them in the halls or cafeteria, but friendship is more than just knowing someone. Having one or two good friends is really worth much more than having a squad of people who simply say "hello" to you in the halls.

Our relationships with people happen on many different levels. There are acquaintances who recognize us and sometimes exchange small talk. They are on the fringe of our lives, very lightly present in our thinking. But they are there.

On another level we can count casual friends, people with whom we've shared some special moments. We have certain interests in common with them, like being in the same classes or working on the same projects. They may be from our neighborhood, or we may have known them in elementary or junior high school. These friends are not now, however, those who share the important things. We may see them at a party or talk with them once in a while, but we don't spend much time with them.

On the highest level—all by themselves—are those super people, the ones who really know us and still like us. Close friends are like icing on the cake of life. They are always there when we need them. They know what we're trying to say before we even find the words, and they are sincerely honest with us. These good friends are genuinely interested in our projects and our sometimes impossible dreams. They cheer us up when we are down and get honestly excited about our successes. They are selfless enough to care about us almost as much as they care about themselves. One—maybe two—good friends are a blessing in anyone's life.

First, Face the Truth

"But I don't need friends," some may say. "I get along by myself. I have friends, sure, but I don't depend on them for anything. I can take care of Number One."

People who talk like this don't have to tell people not to worry about them. No one will! These people have not yet understood the very basic fact that, as the poet John Donne said, "No man is an island."

True, people must be able to stand on their own two feet. Because we are social beings, though, we also need each other. You do need people. Believe as strongly as you can that other people need you, too.

If you're feeling others just don't seem to want your friendship, take a look at yourself. Are you letting people know you respect yourself? Do you give in to peer pressure to use alcohol or drugs as a cheap way of winning friends? Or do you rely on alcohol and/or drugs to escape from life's pressures? Most teens have gotten beyond all those signs of weakness. If they see you involved in those things, they may feel your friendship is not worth having. But if you have a strong sense of self, if you really know who and what you are, that understanding will permeate your whole personality. Others will see this and accept your friendship.

If you are a "poor me" type, who sees yourself as nothing but a loser and a colossal failure at everything including being a human being, you also communicate that feeling to others. Because no one wants to be around such a negative attitude, they won't want to be around you. We all get into this mood sometimes, but it may help if you stop and say to yourself, "Wait a minute. Am I this hard on anyone else? Why should I be this hard on me?"

What Do They Want—My Soul?

No one is asking you to sell your soul or do anything that goes against your personality and character. To be a good friend, however, some things are expected. Sincerity, honesty, generosity, and the ability to give up some of your own pleasure occasionally are necesary for friendship. Friendship is a flexible thing, too. You cannot hold it too tightly, and you cannot even define it. Friendships change. Even if someone is a special friend, don't assume things will remain that way forever.

Friendships grow as people grow, and they change as people change. Good friends, who have enough solid understanding between them, can grow together. This is the same quality that keeps marriages together. Besides being husband and wife, a man and woman must also be best friends. As their lives change, they must be able to keep up with the changes in themselves and each other. If they cannot, they grow in two different directions, and then trouble sets in.

Some Friendships Don't Last

Sometimes friendships end. Some marriages don't last, either. The reason for this may lie in the fact that two people did not grow together, though at one time they had much in common and could share on different levels. One friend, as his or her own personal life evolves, may develop new interests and new values. Suddenly the old friendship seems to be slowly fading, and things don't seem the same anymore.

If this has not happened to you already, you may just as well brace yourself for the first time it does. Since you and others your age are changing so much at this time of your lives, you are bound to develop new interests. You need to develop new interests. And as you mature, some of your values, ideas of fun, and attitudes will change. Your best friend from junior high suddenly may be less friendly, and the two of you may have less to talk about. As a result of these changes, your friendship may be falling apart.

What is happening in this situation is natural. It is something you cannot really stop. The two of you are becoming two individual people, and you are moving in different directions. True, there will be some pain involved as you both go your separate ways. The ending of a friendship is never easy, especially if it was a good friendship. Rather than let the agony of your problem remain and make you uneasy about making other friends, though, just take the good memories of what has been and move on.

Let your friend go free   There is an old proverb that says, "If you love something, set it free. If it comes back, it is yours. If not, it never was." Remember this saying the next time you're tempted to hold onto someone's friendship. You can put your dog on a leash and lock your bike in the garage, but your friends must have the freedom to live their own lives. If the two of you can share your experiences and respect each other's individuality, that's great. If not, you may be good acquaintances, but you are not really good friends.

Trying to hold onto a friendship that has already died can only be a cause of heartache. Accept the pain, try to understand why it happened, and move on. There are other people out there, and once they see an opportunity for friendship with you, they'll come in and fill up any emptiness you may feel.

Cliques Are Not the Answer

The clique is that closely-knit, super popular, very "in" group. It's the easy way to be sure of steady and good friends. Right?

Wrong.

Cliques are a natural for teens who need a lot of people around them. Belonging to a clique means there will always be someone to call on a rainy Saturday and someone who will eat lunch with you in the cafeteria. Belonging to a clique gives a false feeling of security, but it also keeps you from becoming friends with people as individuals.

The false ideal of a true clique is that all members know and like each other equally. Actually, it is just plain impossible to be best friends with four or five different people! Membership in a clique only tends to stifle each individual's personality and keeps him or her from making deeper friendships that can be more personal and lasting.

If being "in" is that important to you, you may be willing to postpone forming deeper friendships for a time. Sooner or later, however, the need for maturity in your own life will take over. One or two people are bound to strike you as people with whom you could share more. You will either have to give up this possibility or remove yourself from the clique.

Keep the door open

High school cliques are nothing more than a carryover from the fifth and sixth grades. That is the stage of child development when it is natural to want to belong to a group. Because children at this age have no developed sense of personal identity, the identity of a group is a good substitute.

As the child moves to adulthood, however, the need for group security should diminish. If it doesn't, you don't really give yourself the chance to learn who you really are as an individual. You don't let yourself learn how you relate to others on a one-to-one basis.

There is nothing wrong with having a crowd of friends—your group, your bunch. When your little group starts getting super exclusive, though, and you notice others staying away from you because they feel you don't want them around, it's time to check a few things. Is your group being cruel to others? Many teen groups do that. Does your group pick fights with others or spend a great deal of energy putting others down? Then there is something wrong with your group, and staying in it is doing some harmful things to you.

One of the greatest opportunities you have in high school is to meet many different kinds of people. If you lock yourself into a tight group that keeps this from happening, you deprive yourself of meeting people who may have a lot more in common with you. In fact, they may have become close friends for life, if you had only given them the chance.

Do yourself a favor. Be open to everyone. Your own group, of course, will exist. Just make sure you let others know there is room for them if they want to be your friends.

Most teens have little respect for adults who lock themselves into fixed routines and then stagnate there. Don't let the same thing happen to you by closing yourself off from the rest of the world with a select group of friends.

Can Adults Be My Friends?

There's no reason why you can't form friendships with adults. Of course, adults are at different stages of their own lives, and many of their interests and values differ from yours. The possibility does remain that a certain teacher, coach, or coworker may strike a responsive chord in you. That could be good. If you can share special problems, or work closely with an adult on a particular project, this may give you an opportunity to get to know him or her in a different way. If this happens, you may find you can really relate to the person, and you can benefit from knowing him or her.

In the adult world, age has little to do with friendship. By realizing that adults are human too, and that you can share with them, you can learn early in life that friendship has more to do with what people have in common than with their age or particular roles in life.

Apple polishing, of course, doesn't make it. It's not honest. A sincere and open attitude, though, can often lead to a better understanding and deeper knowledge of some adults. Don't be intimidated by adults. They may be able to help you, and if you share common ground, they may become your friends, too.

Rapping It Up There are many situations and events that are important in your teen years. People, however, have the greatest power and influence on your life. The people you let into your world, and who spend their time with you, will either help make your high school years positive and productive, or they will make it difficult for you to rise to your full potential.

Cliques won't help you. All they can do is hurt your development as a person. You must choose your friends carefully and individually. Your role as a friend is one of the most important ones you fill. This is true now, and it will be true when you are an adult. If you can learn early to be true to yourself and honest with others, you can take a giant step toward a positive and happy life.

Friendship is one of the most beautiful things in our lives. It can also be one of the most demanding. Friends don't exist to continually feed your ego or constantly back up your every decision, right or wrong. There are always difficult times when two personalities conflict, and you may sometimes feel your friends ask too much of you.

Someone wrote once that friendship is a sacrament that should be taken on one's knees. This is a symbolic way of saying that friendship is almost blessed, and it should be very precious and dear in our lives. Friendships are not prizes we win. They are gifts which should be appreciated and nurtured.

Caring and actually loving is the name of the game. If you can forget your own needs once in a while, and really give part of yourself to another person in honest friendship, you will be able to live up to the standards of true, good relationships. You will also learn how terrific it is to give as well as to take.

Sometime up ahead in your life, you may come to love one person in a special way. The quality of that love you finally are capable of giving in marriage will come partly from the quality of love you learn to give in friendship.

If you don't learn anything else in high school, learn how to be a true friend. You need friendship and so do the people who will be sharing the best and worst times of your life. You are unique and special. Being a good friend to others can make you even more special!

Points to Ponder

1. What qualities about you make you a good friend?

_____

_____

2. How much will you go along with others just to keep their friendship? Be specific.

_____

_____

_____

3. What qualities do you look for in a friend?

_____

_____

_____

4. What do you think holds a real friendship together?

_____

_____

5. Explain your own opinion of cliques.

_____

_____

_____

_____

_____

The Home Front

There's that voice, that very familiar voice, bellowing from the vague direction of the kitchen. "If you don't get out of bed this minute, you'll miss your bus, and you'll have to walk."

Here you go. Another day. Another run-through of all your classes and another chance to face all the pressures that will rear their ugly heads. And where does it all start? At home.

Surviving what happens at school, to no one's surprise, can be made easier or more difficult by the help, or lack of it, that comes from home. Problems at home can affect your whole life. Your success and happiness at home can mean the difference between life being a first-class pain or something that is actually enjoyable.

Understanding the Folks

Your parents never had a class in high school called Parenting 101. And there is no set of standards for achieving super parenthood. Most couples resign themselves to learning how to be good parents mostly by trial and error.

But before you say your folks must be setting the all-time record for errors, try to understand their situation. We have already said it is hard for your folks to keep up with the changes in your life. Even if you are not the first child, you are not a carbon copy of your older brothers and sisters. Because of this, you present a whole new set of problems for Mom and Dad. They never really know what to expect from you. Once they think they do, you pull an about-face and zap them with a whole new way of acting!

If you can understand this, you may be able to understand your parents' reactions a bit better. They need help to understand you, and this is where you can make yourself part of the solution instead of part of the problem. You can give them that help.

Parents aren't perfect

The biggest problem you face with your parents is that they're adults. They are the ultimate authority figures in your life. They have power over you. The state and legal authorities think you are not mature yet. They may be wrong, but they feel you are not responsible for all your actions. So they give your folks rights and responsibilities over your life.

This legal position gives some teens a bitter opinion of their parents. They see their parents as enemies who are standing in the way of their freedom and independence. When these teens feel their freedom is threatened or held back, they resent it, and they resent the people who make it happen.

Don't let that happen to you. The answer, of course, is the growth of understanding between your parents and you. They should realize you are a person on the move, a person who is maturing in many different ways—from your body to your values and abilities. Your parents should also realize that this is their time to begin letting you go. They have to let you test your wings, fall on your face a few times, and finally learn to soar off on an independent and productive life of your own.

You, on the other hand, have to accept the fact that your parents have been your mainstay all these years. Letting go is a painful process. Your folks have really enjoyed watching you grow. You are part of them. Your parents may not be thrilled about paying all the bills your presence has added to the family, but you give them a unique and precious feelings of providing and guiding. Now that they see all these things coming to an end, they have very mixed emotions.

Parents want the best for their children. They want them to be successful and happy. Because of this, your folks are cautious of situations that may be harmful to you. Fearing you might make some gigantic mistakes and wrong decisions, they have rules, guidelines, and, yes, even punishments. Your parents may not be happy about grounding you, but they are acting from the obligation to do what is best for you, whether you understand it or not. If you can understand and begin to respond to your folks in a positive way, chances are they will grant you more freedom and respect in return.

Freedom means no sides

At this point you may be wondering, "Whose side are you on, anyway?" But you shouldn't think in terms of sides.

The family has always been spoken of as a circle. There are no sides in a circle or in a family. There are only people—all of them on the inside.

The adversarial relationship that creeps into too many families comes from any or all of the individuals failing to work together. Selfishness may make you aware of only your side of any problem, and your parents may be equally entrenched in their own views. Arguments and demands that turn a home into a battleground are the result of individuals failing to sit down and honestly appreciate all the aspects of any problem.

How can you avoid confrontation in your own home? You can't. How you attempt to handle that confrontation, however, marks how far you have come along the road to maturity.

Communication Is the Key

There's that word again: communication.

You may think it's impossible to communicate with your parents. You may feel your folks are not interested in your life. They may be up to their ears in their own problems and worries, and because of the time pressures which everyone feels these days, there may be little opportunity to sit down and tell them what's going on. Your parents may also be aware of your growing independence, and they may be trying to avoid meddling in your life. They may not want to appear snoopy, so they may be waiting for you to be the first to talk about certain friends or situations.

Whatever the reasons for the lack of communication, the time to start talking to your parents is now! If you think your parents are uninterested in you, make them interested. Tell them what is important to you, what has you upset, and what worries you. If you think your parents don't care, make them care. They may have reached the point where they are afraid to show some honest affection, or they may be taking you for granted.

Love them. Don't be afraid to let them know they have a special place in your heart. Don't be afraid to give a little hug once in a while. When you were a child, you expected the world to come to you with love and interest. If you really are on your way to adulthood, act like a person who is becoming an adult. Take the initiative. Make the first move. Some members of our society feel awkward about touching and showing affection. But if you cannot show affection in your own way to your family, you're not living your life to the fullest!

Talk!

Talk. Talk. Talk. Don't be afraid to make everyone at home aware of what is happening in your life. Tell them about your classes, about that English teacher who upsets you, about the discussion you had during lunch. Tell them why you like your particular kind of music. Tell them why you wouldn't be caught dead wearing the outfit your aunt gave you for Christmas. Running the risk of boring your family is a much better alternative than running the risk of losing them due to a lack of communication.

Don't be afraid to share with family members. If you do, your parents may soon begin sharing their problems and lives with you. Soon, there you will be—a family, a real family. And you'll be doing what families are supposed to do—care, share, support, and allow growth!

Split Homes—Split Affections

There may be problems at home. You parents may have marital problems, and you may be suffering, too. You may be living with only one of your parents because divorce has split your original family apart. Your family may include stepparents, stepbrothers, and stepsisters. A member of your family may have died. There are a variety of situations that may apply to your family.

You are not alone. Teens today are dealing more often with divorce and remarriage, but people for generations have dealt with these situations. And they have managed to survive well and move on into productive, happy lives.

You first need to understand that any breakups in your family are not your fault. Differences between your mother and father are *theirs*. By trying to understand these differences, you can help each of them move on and make the most of their lives. But in no way should you let the failure of their marriage be a failure for you. It is, in fact, an opportunity for you to show your growing maturity by trying to understand.

If you are now living in a family restructured by remarriage, realize this present group is also your family in every sense of the word. Your stepparent needs your efforts at acceptance. Your stepbrothers and stepsisters also deserve to be part of your life. Be big enough to accept them under the roof and into your heart. They, too, are going through adjustment, and they need to know everyone is making an effort toward becoming a new and caring family.

You should also try to get over being angry with your parents, if they are divorced. If you feel they let you down by separating, you are still very much the child who expects the world to revolve around you. It doesn't. You are part of it; be a positive part of it.

One of the most difficult things you may be expected to realize at this young time of your life is that your parents are human. Because of their own growth and change as individuals, they can no longer share their lives with each other. This is extremely hard to accept, and it is a lot to ask of you. It may, however, be asked of you. Now it is your turn to respond to the situation by showing as much strength and caring as you can.

Recognizing your parents as human beings and facing the reality of their own individuality, you can still love them. You may even be living apart from one or both of them. But they are still family, and they always will be. If you can enjoy your good memories and think of your parents in a positive way all through your life, you will have a richness no one can ever destroy. If your parents have hurt you, be strong enough to forgive them. None of you is perfect.

Family is for sharing. If you are going to share the good, you know you are also expected to share the bad. It is never easy, but sad times are part of every individual's growth as a person. If you do your best to work through them, you will develop a sense of strength and accomplishment that you can carry with you into your adult life.

Brothers and Sisters

In thinking about your home front, you must also consider your brothers and sisters. They can present a real problem for you, or they can be a real joy. Sure, you may resent your older brother because he seems to have had it so much easier than you. You may even detest the way your little stepsister keeps interrupting you when your friends are over, or you're trying to listen to music or work.

Living with someone is not the easiest thing in the world. In the case of brothers and sisters, there is always the temptation to compare how they are treated with how you think you are making out. You may think they get their way more often than you do. Yet passing up the chance to develop a good relationship with brothers and sisters may be one of the biggest mistakes you can make. They are individuals. They are going through their own stages, and they may need all the understanding you can give. Your brothers and sisters will be very special people throughout your life, and they can become unique friends when you are all adults.

Family relationships are things that never stop. If you can keep yourself on good terms with your brothers and sisters now, you may find that your older brother will be a good friend and ally in years to come. Your little stepsister, once she is a woman, will be a source of pride and sincere joy for you.

By sharing your own successes and interests in school, you can help your younger brothers and sisters have a better attitude toward education. Also, by confiding in your older brothers and sisters, you can learn a lot and make them feel useful. Even that kid brother who may be a pain now will be a good friend in the future, so give him some understanding and love.

Rapping It Up

The school has an open house, and only a handful of parents appear. Why? There may be many answers. Mom and Dad are too busy. Or they may not care. Mom and Dad would have come, but you never told them about it. Mom and Dad wanted to come, but you told them if they went, you would jump out your bedroom window!

You, your home, and your school are all wound up in an interesting and complicated maze. You can keep each part of your life very separate, and never share a word about one with the other. Or you can let what happens in school and at home flow into each other. You can help your teachers understand you better by letting them in on some of the aspects of your home life. Also, you can make home an easier place to come back to by not keeping school happenings a military secret.

Your parents are human. They have their own lives, and they are unique individuals. They are also the people who have the greatest possibility of influencing your life. If you let them, their influence can be terrific.

Do you realize that your ties to home can be your biggest asset during high school? Honest communication with your folks can give your home life a whole new dimension. It can also give you some valuable help with your problems.

If there are walls between you and your parents, or between you and your brothers and sisters, tear them down with honest communication. You may actually be the one who will turn things around at home and make everyone else more open and caring, as well as more interested in each other.

You certainly are not a "kid" anymore. You know it. Begin to assume a bit more responsibility on the home front by taking the initiative when things need to get done and by accepting responsibility for some of the family's concerns. These actions will go a long way toward proving to your parents that you are not "that selfish kid" anymore.

Your folks are watching you, and waiting. Every hint that you are turning into a more open and dependable individual is a joy to them. Every time you experience failure, so do they. By sharing with them, you can help them understand how you're doing and give them some clues to help you become a better person.

Home is where the heart is; you will love many other people and things in your life, but you should always leave room for your family. They have been with you in these early years, and you will have more going for you if you keep them close in the years to come. Good relationships with your family will help you build better relationships with others as you enter the adult world on your own.

Points to Ponder   1. How much emotional support do you get from your family?

_____

_____

_____

2. What are your parents' biggest concerns right now?

    _____

    _____

    _____

3. How open are you with your parents?

    _____

    Give an example of your honesty with them, or your
    lack of it.

    _____

    _____

    _____

4. How important is home to you?

    _____

    How different will your own home be when you have a
    family? Be specific.

    _____

    _____

    _____

    _____

    _____

The Free Spirit in Free Time

12

"Don't bother opening up the curtain for my social scene," you might say. "There's no one on the stage!"

What most people would call your social life, and what you might sometimes feel like calling a disaster, includes all that time when you're pretty much your own boss. True, you have homework, family responsibilities, and curfews, but how you fill up free hours is becoming more and more your own decision.

There does come a joyous time when the last class is over, and you can head into those streets that are so familiar to you. You are free at last. You are on your own, and you finally have a chance to do whatever you want!

Hard as a Rock Concert

What you choose for entertainment says much about you. The people you spend time with also have an effect on you.

Entertainment, if you can face this fact, means more to

you than it does to many adults. They have more things to fill up their lives, and their free time is limited. Most adults face responsibilities, pressures, and concerns from which you are still relatively free. Entertainment for adults is really a time to escape from their problems and relax.

Teens, however, because they are so involved with peer pressure and because they cannot escape the fact that their lives are changing, tend to think of their social lives as something to enjoy, but also something to *work* on. Don't fall into the trap of forcing yourself to have fun or be happy. Relaxing is the first key to really enjoying your free time.

Most adults would go crazy at a rock concert. They may not understand that, for you, being where the action is means being active.

Ah, but look at yourself at a concert! What a sight! Are you going to sit back and just let all that good music go to waste? Absolutely not! There you are—dancing, clapping, singing, and getting so involved with it all that no one can tell where the music stops and you start. You are really into it, and you love every minute!

It's great that you can enjoy that special spark inside you that makes you act this way. Just don't *make* yourself do it. The first answer to entertainment is being yourself.

Hanging Out

Of course, not all your time is going to be spent at organized entertainment functions such as dances, movies, and concerts. You probably can't afford it, and, besides, there is a lot to be said for just "hanging out" with your friends. Don't be afraid to spend time doing "nothing productive" with your buddies. You need these free times, when you are not facing any pressures of role or image. You probably know some adults who are so caught up in their roles that they can't be themselves. If they could just sit back, as you should, and let their friends accept them as they are, they would be better off.

Be careful not to fall into the trap of image, even in your free time. If you feel you have to be seen in the right places with the right people, doing the right things, you may be winning points in the popularity poll, but you may not be true to youself. You may not be truly happy, either. Your free-time activities show you very clearly as you really are. Let them be natural and unpressured.

The School Connection

Some teens feel they are living on an island, with nothing to do and no one to share their time. If you feel this way, look back at chapter 8 on extracurricular involvement and review the main idea.

Part of your education is in the books, but a big part of it is in the things you do outside the classroom. This includes the many activities that are sponsored by the school and that are either free or very economical. If you feel there is nothing to do in the evenings, involvement in a play, a club, or a special school activity could take care of that problem. It could also put you in contact with some interesting and stimulating people.

Your social life can get its biggest push from your connection with school and the people you met there. Don't be afraid to give it a try.

Dating or Waiting?

"When should I start dating? What's the right age? How do I know when I'm ready?"

No one can answer those questions for you. There are, of course, many people who will try. Your folks may have some very definite ideas about it. Your teachers may offer advice, and certainly your friends will put the pressure on you to move ahead into this possibly exciting time of your life. But when is the right time for you? Only you know for sure.

Some parents, wanting success for their children in all areas of their lives, will push their sons and daughters to date very early. They may feel they missed out on the action when they were young, and therefore they want their children to have the fun and popularity they missed. Other parents fear the worst and want to keep their children on the shelf until they reach twenty!

Whether you are a boy or a girl, some good, honest discussion with your folks may help get these issues settled. Whatever you do, don't let yourself be pushed into doing anything you feel is not right for you. Your parents will get over the fact that right now you may be more interested in watching football games than dating. They will also survive that fateful night when you do walk out the front door on your first date. There will probably have to be some compromises on both sides, but your dating life should grow directly out of your readiness for it and your honest desire to begin dating.

Your peers, the gang at school, may also try to force their own ideas on you. If they think you are ready to date, but you just don't feel like it, let them know in an independent but kind way that you are still thinking about it. If they are your real friends, they will back off and leave you alone on that subject for a while.

Inventory Choose the answers that best describe you.

____ I need someone to be there just for me.

____ My folks don't understand what I need.

____ Dating is my right whenever I choose.

____ It's time I got sexually active, so why not?

____ My friends date, so I might as well, too.

Guess what? All these attitudes have one thing in common. None of them shows a healthy, open attitude toward dating. If you checked any of them, go back to the drawing board and rethink your attitudes, needs, and reasons for wanting to date.

Dancing queen—or turning green?

Ah, that first date!

Dan is there, spiffed up until his hair squeaks. Debbie comes down the stairs, her eyes full of stars. And they are off for the evening.

Mom and Dad watch them drive away, thinking back to their own teenage years. Dad immediately buries his head in the newspaper. He's not reading it; he's trying to cope with the fact that his little girl has just walked out the door.

At the restaurant Dan is the epitome of politeness, and Debbie, after ordering, sits anxiously back and looks at him.

Silence. Very horrible, awkward silence! Now what? Panic time! What to say?

Cheer up. Your first date, or your first meeting with anyone who has the potential of becoming special to you, will have its awkward moments. The possibilities are so great, and the situation so new, that it will always take a little time to adjust. But that old standby, communication, will come to your aid again. Sure, you may have to ask some foolish, seemingly superficial questions. You may even end up giving a dissertation on a class at school. Eventually, however, you will loosen up if you are both talking.

Silence is a beautiful thing when it happens between

two people who know each other so well they can be comfortable with it. Until that happens, words are going to be your best bet. Disc jockeys fight to avoid the number one disaster in radio—dead air. It is a horrible moment when nothing is happening. Nothing is being said or sung. It is considered a failure for them. Likewise, until you can learn to share meaningful silence with someone in a special situation such as a date, try learning about the other person's interests. Avoid your own dead air. Ask "why" and "how" questions that will require more than a "yes" or "no" answer. Keep believing that—sooner or later—the ice will break. If the communication is open and honest, you both should begin to have a good time.

Dating can ruin your social life

How can this be?

Take a moment to think about your total social life, which includes all those faithful friends who were the mainstay of your free time before Mr. or Miss Wonderful came along. Some teens, once they start dating, quickly forget their old friends and neglect them. This, of course, is one of the surest ways of missing out on a lot of fun. It also marks you as a friend who will be around only until something better comes along, and that's not good.

It is possible to date and still maintain a schedule for doing things with your other friends from time to time. The more you become involved with one person, the more difficult it will be to maintain this balance. However, it's important to try. You owe it to yourself, and you owe it to the friends who have stood by you when things weren't as rosy as they may be now.

Steady Freddy

Many teens today feel that once they begin dating, they cannot, or must not, even look at another member of the opposite sex. But going out with a person a couple of times does not mean he or she *owns* you. Guys are notorious for being very possessive of their girlfriends. Also, some girls become very jealous if they see their boyfriend even saying "Hi" to another girl.

Possessiveness, like it or not, is just a way of keeping a kind of social security. "Going steady" is not really preparing for marriage in most cases. It is simply making sure that you will have a date for the big dance, or that Saturday night will not be a lonely, miserable evening with your little brother.

Some more mature couples who can realize this will loosen up in their relationships and agree to date other people. If you can handle this, do it. The teen years are a time for finding out what life has to offer. It usually is not wise to plan your future around the first person you date. Perhaps some marriages fail because the partners did not date enough in their teens. They got so involved with each other, so early, that they never really learned of others who also could have been good life partners. You may even ask that question of your own parents if they have divorced.

Group dating is also returning to the social scene. This arrangement, which was common several decades ago, involves several different boys and girls meeting at one place and having a good time together. There is no great emphasis on pairing off. There is just an open, good evening of fun. Eventually, of course, couples may begin to form. However, for a while, this arrangement gives everyone a chance to get to know many different kinds of people. It also helps you make some decisions about one-to-one dating with a little more intelligence and understanding. Try it. You might like it.

Is sex part of dating? That's a question that you, as a young person, must answer for yourself. Music, films, and locker room discussions will tell you sex is always part of dating. The honest people who want to date, even with the same person for quite a while, will tell you that it isn't.

While we'll talk about sexual involvement in a later chapter, let's say this much right now. Society today seems to say that sex is all right for anyone, anytime. In too many high schools and colleges, young people give the impression that it is as common an occurrence as going to a restaurant. They may tell you sex is the natural ending to any night of socializing.

They are wrong. And they are wrong not just because AIDS is a real concern these days. They are wrong not only because sexual involvement before marriage violates many people's religious beliefs. They are wrong simply because if you are a healthy, independent person, no one can tell you what is right for *you*.

Many young people have even stopped dating simply because they don't want to constantly fight off the pressure for sex. Don't get caught up in the idea that sex is part of dating. It is not. When you do start dating, show your maturity and growth of independence by your actions. Dating does not mean going to bed with anyone who has given you a meal, smiled at you nicely, or told you you're special.

Be really special. Be your own person, and make your own decisions.

Rapping It Up   Your friends can be the source of much fun and real enjoyment. You can even learn to have some good times with your family, if you are open and communicative at home. And your school is set up to provide many activities that you can enjoy after regular class hours. In fact, your whole life—if you let it—can become a source of real pleasure and fulfillment. Being open with others and honest with yourself is the key.

Dating can give you valuable experience in learning how to handle personal relationships. It can open your eyes to the wonderful world of caring in a special way, and it can make you more aware of yourself as a worthwhile individual. Being loved is one of the greatest ego builders around. Just remember to let dating, and your social life in general, come easily and comfortably for you. Don't let anyone pressure you into doing things that make you feel uncomfortable.

If you can learn to smile at life, you may soon find it smiling back at you. Enjoy!

Points to Ponder   1. How much does the entertainment you choose reflect the real you?

   _____

   _____

   2. How able are you to forget your image and really be yourself when you are out for the evening?

   _____

   Why is this true? _____

   _____

3. How can you keep your old friends once you start dating on a fairly regular basis?

_____

_____

_____

4. Can you be yourself on a date, or do you feel you must always please the other person?

_____

_____

5. What are your own attitudes toward sexual involvement?

_____

_____

_____

_____

A Sporting Chance

13

Five seconds left on the clock! The score is tied! Wait, there goes the quarterback! He's going to pass! It's long, long. Murphy is there. He's reaching—Yes! Touchdown! The crowd goes wild!

Sports can be like that, and sports can be very different. There is a lot of glory on a playing field, a basketball court, or a track. Some teens, thinking they can get a piece of it, sign up for a team. Participating in any sport, however, also involves a lot of behind-the-scenes work and hours of lonely, hard training. The few minutes of individual glory that may follow are never ensured. Often, the person who goes out for a team just to win the praise of others does not last too long.

Is It Worth It? This is a question you must answer for yourself. Participating in your high school sports program certainly offers many opportunities for growth, if you are willing to pay the price. Working at sports—and it certainly is work and not play—can tone up your body while also toning up your mind. The training and sense of dedication which will be demanded of you will teach you how to give yourself to a worthy goal. By competing, you can learn the valuable lesson that *trying* is often more rewarding than any victory that may come.

No athlete who is worthy of continued support looks at glory as the goal. To excel in sports, a person must really enjoy putting out the best effort at all times. He or she knows the personal satisfaction that can come from reaching individual goals. Even though an athlete works hard to win, the most important winning goes on inside the person. It is the personal best, not the all-time, all-mighty best, which really counts.

Whether or not you decide to participate in high school sports will depend heavily on your own evaluation of what is important. You have only so much time. If sports is that important to you, then make the commitment to do it well.

How Important Is Winning?

Ron is out for football. He enjoys it. His dad, the number one fan of all time, is behind him 100 percent. Dad tries to make as many practice sessions as he can. And when a game is coming up, he helps Ron review the patterns and plays, as well as the scouting reports.

Sounds great, right? Yet when Ron fumbles the football during the big game, and the home team goes on to lose by one touchdown, it is not Ron, but Dad, who goes to pieces. "How could he do that? My son? How could he do that to me?" Now that story doesn't sound so great because Ron, like many other teens, is getting too much pressure from the home front.

Many students, both boys and girls, choose not to go out for sports in high school because they feel they can't take the pressure, either from their own parents or from other sources. You may ask, "What pressure? It's only a game." This is the attitude some teens take, but other students fear the tension they might feel if they got involved in sports. Rather than bring that problem into their lives, these teens stay away from competitive sports.

In some school systems, the athletic program is extremely important. It is a very visible way for the parents and taxpayers to see something tangible about the high school. Some school officials feel that if the rugged football team is not winning, the high school as a whole is not winning at anything, either. This, of course, is not true. When parents of school athletes or school personnel make winning conference titles and championships the most important thing, trophy fever is quickly transmitted to the coaches and the players. Tension builds. Look at the frequency with which coaches at schools change jobs. If they last only a couple of years, you can be sure there is pressure from somewhere to win, and win big.

The secret of participating in varsity sports, where this pressure will always be present to some degree, is to let it remain in the background as an incentive to do better. It should never overshadow the real purpose of the sporting program. If some adults in the community get upset about losing once in a while, that is their problem. Don't let it become yours as well.

The importance of sports is always a good question for debate. Some teens feel it is treated like the only thing going on in the school. Others feel it is not given enough support. The way you feel about this issue may change during your high school career, but traveling the middle road will always give you the best perspective. No one thing is all-important in high school. The whole concept of secondary education lies in providing as many experiences as possible for as many people as possible. If sports is your interest, then go for it, and give it the best you can. If you choose not to participate on the varsity level, there are always less-pressured teams that compete more for enjoyment and do not carry the reputation of the school on their backs.

Team Sports   If you decide to become involved in sports, you will have to decide on the type of competition you desire. The sports that usually capture much of the glory, and much of the fans' money, are the team efforts. Basketball and football remain the two favorites in most high schools. Swimming, hockey, and soccer are also quickly gaining support in different areas of the country.

Team sports involve a particular kind of pressure. Each individual has his or her own assignment and becomes a specialist. An athlete plays one position or participates in only one or two events. He or she then must concentrate on a very narrow aspect of the total game. Excellence, if a player achieves it, is to be outstanding in his or her unique job.

The greatest satisfaction for you as a team player, if you decide to become involved, will be to learn to work with others for a common goal—victory. Team effort will continue on many different levels all through life, such as in your job and in your family. If you can learn to sacrifice yourself once in a while for the greater good of the group, you will have learned a lot!

Individual Sports

"I'd rather be in a sport where I can control everything. In each event, I am the only one I have to worry about. I know if I can do everything as well as I can, I have a good chance of winning. Each time I compete against my own performance at the last meet. This way I know if I'm getting any better."

A state champion in gymnastics said that, and her feelings are echoed by both men and women who participate in singles tennis, weightlifting, golf, and other individual sports. These sports, fulfilling to the person who chooses them, demand another kind of training. In these games you will be expected to learn all the aspects of the sport. When the competition starts, it is you who will succeed or fail. Some teens find the pressure of these sports a bit much to handle. If something goes wrong, there is no one else to blame.

This kind of pressure requires an individual who is self-confident enough to go out and attempt the best. Very few teens who participate in individual sports are shy or have personality problems. They have to be in control of their emotions as well as their bodies. These athletes must really have their act together, both mentally and physically.

If you choose to try out for a sport that will put you all alone against the rest of the world, you know something about yourself. You are not afraid of failure. You are a confident and psychologically strong individual, or you will soon be!

Consider Other Alternatives

While many teens choose not to get involved with varsity sports, they still take advantage of sports as hobbies and fun-filled activities. From learning tennis just for enjoyment to playing in an intramural program, sports still have much to offer.

Consider joining a bowling league in your neighborhood, or studying gymnastics or modern dance at a local studio. Jogging or power walking are popular sports that you can take into your adult life. In northern areas, cross-country skiing, or other winter sports, always ensure hours of fun with people who share your common interests. Also, there are many teens who get into the habit of working out, either in a weight or an aerobics program at a local fitness center. An interest in exercise is not only good now. It will give you a healthy attitude toward your body and can continue through adult life.

Just remember that you don't have to be part of the varsity program at school to enjoy sports. Find what's good for you and enjoy it!

Rapping It Up

There are many levels of sporting competition available to you in high school. Even in gym class you will have a chance to learn aspects of different sports. You may develop an interest in some sports that will last for years to come.

Sandlot games and intramural competition are a lot of fun. Individual sports such as bowling, tennis, and running offer healthy and enjoyable recreation. They will give you a good workout. And, although you will be more responsible for your own performance, in these sports you won't have to face the pressure that comes with highly visible varsity teams.

High school is your big job right now. It is there for developing the total you. Whether you are fond of it or not, your body will be with you all your life. If you don't give it a chance to develop through healthy exercise during your teens, you may find it wearing out on you much sooner than you had expected.

Participation in sports can also help you learn to use your leadership abilities well. Many high schools look to their varsity players for initiative and leadership, simply because they know these people know how to face challenges.

If you choose to become involved in high school sports programs, give them your best. Also, remember that the pressure is only a tool that can help you give even more than you thought posible.

If, on the other hand, you decide that sports are not for you, don't judge those who do participate. Athletes are proving to themselves and the rest of the world that they can be a success in any field. They are asserting their individuality by putting their own effort on the line and by striving for victory in their own ways. Any individual who participates in sports is asserting himself or herself by that choice. If some of your friends elect to dedicate themselves to the discipline of sports, respect the courage and stamina they show, and give them your support.

You can, of course, expect the same kind of respect from your sports-minded friends when you get involved in drama, music, journalism, or debate. High school is really one big team, and if you can learn to pull together with everyone—respecting them for their individuality and asserting yourself at the same time—you can work through any prejudices or pressures which may come along. All it takes is remembering to be a good sport!

Points to Ponder

1. Do you feel capable of the real dedication it takes to participate in school sports?

_____

_____

Explain why you do or don't like sports.

_____

_____

2. How well can you handle the pressure of competition?

_____

_____

Can you lose once in a while without falling apart? Explain.

_____

_____

3. It takes a lot of faith in one's ability to enter competition. How much faith in yourself do you have?

_____

_____

4. If you do not participate in sports, are you open-minded toward the people who do? If you do participate, are you supportive of friends with other extracurricular interests? Give examples.

_____

_____

_____

_____

The Battle for the Buck

14

There he is, in the locker room. Bill has a few minutes alone before the rest of the guys come in. Suddenly he realizes a lot of wallets are lying around, unprotected and very vulnerable. The opportunity is there. Chances are Bill may not be caught, and there is that tape he was was looking at in the store just last Saturday. Tempting. Very tempting. What will our man Bill do? What would you do?

No one will deny that having money is important. Money is simply a necessary thing. Without it, our entire lives would be very different. Our possession of it, or our lack of it, may determine what others think of us. The need for money may add to the tension at home. And it may force us to pass up participation in after-school activities in order to work at a part-time job.

Money can be a problem.

I Need Some Money!

Everyone needs money. So, how can you get it? And what is enough for you?

Teens who are too young to be hired in the business world are often frustrated. Baby-sitting can be one alternative to empty pockets. Or, enterprising young teens can investigate the opportunites for offering lawn care and home maintenance services in their area.

Unfortunately, stealing is another possibility for many. No high school administrator can say that his or her school is free from theft problems. Often, stealing is considered the number one crime of teenagers. Lockers are not vaults. In older buildings, it is easy to break into them. Many students are careless with purses and wallets. As a result, the temptation to help themselves to the contents of those things is almost unbearable for some students.

If you ever face such a temptation, aware of your need for money and the ease with which you might get it, there is only one thing that can make that decision for you. Your conscience will be the final judge, and your own set of priorities and values will make the right answer clear.

As was mentioned earlier, all of your actions are the direct result of what you think is important. If having money means winning popularity and the envy of others, you may decide to steal it. If no higher values come into play, your conscience may take a back seat and make room for what you decide is most important. That is sad, but it happens many times in high schools today. How you act depends solely on you. No one can make a rule you will obey or set a guideline you will follow if you first cannot set your own values right. Religion, strict parents, or watchful teachers can't control you. You can, and do, make all your own decisions.

Because the world is as it is, we must also face the temptation of some teens to be pushers of various kinds of drugs in their own schools or neighborhoods. This is not only wrong and a crime. It is despicable because these few teens are aiding and abetting the drug habits and destruction of their fellow teens. Drug dealers use their own need for more and more money to ruin the lives of their classmates and families. If you know anyone like that, get them out of your school and off the street. If you have a temptation to become one of them, consider the person most precious to you. Would you sell drugs to that person? Would you put him or her through the hell that involvement with drugs eventually brings?

One of the most essential things you have to develop during high school is a realistic and honest attitude toward money. Money is a tool, and that's all. True, it is a handy tool to have around, but if it becomes more than that, you may end up being a very frustrated and miserable human being.

How about Allowances?

Do high school students need money in their pockets? Of course they do. If you or your friends have parents who don't believe it, be sure you let them know what real life is all about. As you mature, you need to feel you are developing your own independence. Anything that can help that feeling of being able to handle your own life should be yours.

Every teen should be able to feel the security of knowing that he or she will not be embarrassed by being unable to meet the little needs that can appear. There may be a new paperback you need for English class, or your friends may decide to stop for a snack after school. It doesn't have to be much, but you should feel the confidence of knowing you can handle most normal money demands.

The amount of money you carry, of course, can get to be another story. If you always feel you need fifty dollars in your pocket "just in case," you may be spending too much money. Several dollars will usually do the trick, and carrying them will give you a better understanding of money. Watching those dollars disappear will make you think twice before you decide you really need something. It may also teach you to look for bargains.

How Much Is Enough?

You may be very aware of a member of your crowd who always has a lot of money. This person is always willing to pay for that after-school cheeseburger. When he or she opens up that wallet, it makes you feel like a pauper.

Some teens, whose parents are well off, carry large amounts of cash. They may use money as an image builder, and they may derive some of their confidence in social situations from their ability to pay. However, most teens do not have the opportunity to build their images in this manner, and, actually, they're better off. Relying on money for friendship or prestige is a trap in which many adults are caught, too. If you can avoid this feeling while you are young, so much the better.

There is no set amount of allowance that is right for everyone. Some areas of the country are more expensive than others. Also, some teens face more financial pressures than others. Everyone's need for the bothersome buck is different, and this has to be considered.

Your biggest consideration, however, should come from your family. As a small child, you may have had an unrealistic idea of how much money they had. You usually got what you wanted, and maybe there always seemed to be a few extra dollars in your mother's purse. Part of growing up, though, is realizing the truth about your family's financial situation.

Your parents may be having a hard time paying the rent or mortgage each month. In addition, both you and your parents are probably very aware of prices that keep going up and up. A good, honest talk with your parents about finances should give you a more realistic idea of whether you can expect a large allowance, or if your family needs all its income for basic expenses. Your folks may already be cutting back on their own expenses. If this is the case, you should try to understand and imitate their example since you are now a more mature, responsible member of the family.

Your parents are putting out a lot of money for you in many different ways. They may also be saving for your college years and the enormous expenses that time will bring. Understanding some of your parents' expenses will give you a better appreciation of what they are facing. It may also prompt you to rethink your life-style. Sharing family problems is a job for all mature members of the household. If you want to feel you are growing up, don't miss the opportunity to start taking charge of your own finances.

You May Need a Job

Are part-time jobs good for teens? That's a good question with a complicated answer.

Some parents don't want their sons and daughters to work while they are in high school. They feel school work might suffer. Others, facing the straining family budget, honestly tell their children that a little extra added income would help. These parents encourage their teens to go out and find jobs.

Teenagers' needs tend to get more expensive, too. Buying a small toy for little Susan isn't too bad. But when Susan is in the market for some good stereo equipment, things get more complicated.

Part-time jobs do have benefits. They can be a real learning experience. Jobs give young people a chance to work with others of different ages and backgrounds. They also offer the opportunity to become involved in the work world, with all its challenges and rewards. Some teens feel they learn a lot by working. Book knowledge gives them a basis for thinking about future career possibilities. However, the experience gained from slinging hamburgers gives them more confidence to handle real-life situations.

One danger of working is the possibility that your study time will be reduced. Work may also cut into free time, which you need. If your job gets so hectic that you are running home from school, giving your homework a lick and a promise, and then rushing off to a job, you are missing a very important time in your life. You need time to hang loose—to relax. If you don't get this time, you may join the thousands of teens who are trying to get rid of ulcers. If your job creates a situation like that, it's not worth it.

Teens usually work very hard and get paid minimum wage or less. You are the last to be hired and the first to be fired. You are at rock bottom on the pay scale. If you can face this and still work for the extra money you may feel will make your life more comfortable, go to it. Don't let a job get in the way of what is important in your life, though. Your education and your growth as a person should always come first.

The dazzle of a fairly large paycheck has driven many teens out of school before graduation. Most soon found out, however, that they were making money, but were also stuck in jobs with little opportunity for advancement. As a result, they faced a lifetime of really hard work.

Stay in school. Work if you must, but keep your priorities straight. The world does not owe you a living, but you owe yourself the chance to make the most of your potential.

Rapping It Up

There are a lot of well-dressed adults who may make you green with envy because of the cars they drive and the image of success they project—because of their money.

Although pleased with themselves and their possessions, some of these people have little else of real satisfaction in their lives. They are hung up on material things, on possessing things, on working for more money to buy more things. As a result, these people end up with little time to enjoy life, and with houses full of things.

Money is great, but it certainly isn't everything. It may give you a feeling of superiority or success. However, when you get down to the bottom line of meeting and dealing with people, it is *you* who will make the final impression. Your personality, your values, and your ability to respect yourself as a human being will lead others to their final judgements about you.

If money can take a realistic and proper place as your priorities develop, you will be a much happier and more contented adult. Your high school years and your enjoyment of them will be much richer, too.

Points to Ponder

1. Do you feel you have a realistic attitude toward money? _____ How important is money to you? Be specific.

_____

_____

2. How would you advise a friend who is tempted to steal?

_____

_____

_____

3. How well do you understand your family's financial position?

_____

How can you accept those limits?

_____

_____

4. How many hours a week do you think a high school student should work at a part-time job? How would you make time for a job right now?

_____

_____

_____

5. How much money do you feel you need each month? Be specific, and explain where the money will be going.

_____

_____

_____

_____

_____

Pressures, Problems, and Possibilities

No matter how much advice you get on how things should go during your high school years, the fact remains that there are many problems you will have to face. In fact, the way you face any pressure or problem is a big description of you as a person. It shows how strong you have become since you entered your teens and whether you are still a "kid."

There are those who say people never know their true character until a difficult situation arises. That's when we find out what we're "made of." Let's make an attempt at finding out what you are "made of."

Let's Take a Look   In the spaces on the next page, write a one-sentence answer about how you think you might react to the situation described. Be as honest as you can.

1. Your friend is thinking of committing suicide. You see many of the signs, and you fear this may not be an act. What do you do?

   _____

   _____

2. Some people you know decide to make your life miserable by putting you down and telling lies about you behind your back. What is your reaction?

   _____

   _____

3. You feel your friends are, more and more, making you do things you really don't want to do. What is your reaction?

   _____

   _____

4. On a scale of 1–10, 10 being the highest, rate your personality. Describe your strong points and your weaknesses.

   _____

   _____

   _____

   _____

   _____

5. What two things could you do to increase your ability to deal with problems?

   _____

   _____

   _____

You May Be Your Biggest Problem

Your attitude toward yourself may be the cause of some of your most difficult problems. If this is so, it *is* possible to improve the situation.

First, let's consider your body. You may feel no one would especially want to do that, and you may be right. Are you concerned about your weight or about some physical feature you feel may be turning people off? If so, something in your attitude toward others may be letting people know you are unhappy about yourself. You are at a time of life when you may be overly concerned about your looks and your body. If not checked, this concern could turn into a big problem for you.

If some feature about your body makes you insecure, it may make you louder than you should be. You may feel you have to be more fun to be with, so that people will like you. You may go to the other extreme and retreat into a shell, feeling you then can shut yourself off from any possibilities of rejection. Either way, your body is part of you. If you don't like it, or are not comfortable with some aspect of it, you may be in for some problems.

Learn to Accept, Except . . .

No one goes through life these days without watching television, but you ought to be aware that it can give you some very false ideas. You may have fallen into the trap of thinking all teens should look like the fresh, blond actors who advertise everything from acne medications to toothpaste. The cable and network sit-coms have many good-looking guys and girls who are not only making a lot of money, but who are also the envy of many people their own age. But these actors are themselves. You are you.

Try watching the news instead of the comedies or the commercials. On the news, you will see the real world being interviewed on the spot. You will begin to realize that the ideal world of people we see on the sit-coms and commercials is not reality.

Learning to feel comfortable with your body means accepting what you cannot change and honestly trying to do something about those things you can control. Braces, acne, and some baby fat may be part of the territory right now, but they are not permanent. A good look at acne medicines or a trip to a dermatologist may at least get acne under control. Braces have become so common and inconspicuous that if you let them be a problem to you, you are just not noticing that half of your classmates also have them. Just think of that million dollar smile you'll have someday! Likewise, you may feel your body is not maturing as quickly as those of your friends or the other guys or girls in the locker room. That may be a problem now, but people develop at their own pace. Your adult body will take its true form soon enough.

You may not like your nose, your eyes, or your ears. You may detest the fact that you inherited the family chin. You may be miserable about the curl, or lack of it, in your hair. But these are the features that make you who you are. As soon as you begin to accept them as part of your own uniqueness, you can begin to feel comfortable with yourself. You are not a carbon copy of a television commercial, and that is what is so terrific about you! You are an individual, and you look like an individual.

Leave the house each morning looking your best. If you are clean and put together as well as you can be, you have done all that is possible. If others cannot accept how you look, that is their problem. It is not yours.

It's All in My Mind

Another problem you may face during your teens is the fear that you are not intelligent enough. One of the worst things anyone can say to a high school student is "You're stupid" or "You're dumb."

With all the pressure for grades and the emphasis on success, you may feel you cannot cope. You may fear the SAT scores when they come back, or the other standardized tests that have come to mean so much when it comes to college acceptance. A talk with your counselor will help. You have a right to see the results of I.Q. tests and other scholastic achievement scores. That is the law. Ask to see them and then ask your counselor to help you evaluate and understand your scores. In this way you can get a realistic idea of your abilities and possible weaknesses. You can begin to put forth more effort in areas where you need it and start to be more comfortable with your own level of intelligence. You can also begin to use your scores to discover various careers for which you're well suited.

Personality—Plus or Total Zero?

If someone asked you to draw a picture of your personality, would you produce a blank piece of paper? Guess what? Many people are not totally happy with their personalities, either. Other than the supreme egotist, the majority of people usually feel there is something lacking in the way they relate to others. That really is not a problem. Instead, it represents a very healthy frame of mind, since it makes most people try harder to be a bit more interested in others.

Your personality comes from the essential *you*, the person you began to discover in the first few chapters of this book. The way you react, either as a thinker, a doer, a leader, or a producer, will determine your personality. As an extrovert, you may feel comfortable taking charge of situations and conversations. You may feel more secure in a group. If you are a more thoughtful type, you may choose to sit back and let others take the initiative while you get a better view of situations. You may need time alone once in a while just to sort things out. That's fine, as long as the time alone doesn't claim more and more of your life. That could be a danger sign.

In whatever way you react, your basic personality must be geared toward others. The different ways you communicate with them and respond to them will give them their only clues to your real identity. If you can honestly be yourself, your personality will evolve very naturally and comfortably for you and the people you meet. In some writing classes, students often express a desire to develop a writing style. Any good teacher will give the best advice: the more the writer develops as a person, the more his or her writing style will develop, since writing is simply putting yourself and your thoughts on paper.

No one is "up" all the time, and it is not normal for anyone always to be miserable. Your moods will swing back and forth; that's only human. The secret lies in not letting one mood grab hold of you and stay too long. Sickness, sadness, and even death will come into your life as you care for the people you love. Feeling periods of sadness or mourning those who have died is human, and an act of love for them. But refusing to put them and the past into perspective can be the beginning of real psychological problems. If you can stay open to yourself and others and keep a positive attitude, you can soon get on top of any mood and let the normal happiness of life take over again. Even mourning ends in time.

Do you want a good personality? Just be the *you* that makes you feel most comfortable, sincere, and human. The honest person is a breath of fresh air in our society. Be one, and let others share that open, sunny feeling when they meet you.

Pressure Is a Real Pain! Too much pressure certainly is a pain. A realistic look at high school life, though, is going to reveal all kinds of pressure, whether you like it or not. The secret to dealing with pressure is in learning how to cope with it and learning how to relieve it.

If a big exam is approaching and has you in a state of panic, there are several ways to deal with it. You can tell everyone you know about it, complain about it, and make sure any person within forty feet knows you are worried out of your mind about it. Good approach? No way. All this will do is reinforce your own feelings of tension and invite others to be tense with you. Not only will you feel pressured, but your whole class will begin to feel like a crew of astronauts waiting for the end of the countdown.

Another approach involves taking a hard look at why this test has you so tense. Is it really that important? Are the results going to be as earth-shattering as you make them out to be?

If the answer is "yes," you should study as calmly and thoroughly as you can. Arrange a work session with others so you can compare notes. Then simply do your best. Understanding and dealing with sources of pressure is a way of succeeding in high school. And, if you can learn to handle stress during your teens, your adult life will be a lot simpler. You will also save a lot of money on ulcer medicine.

Peer pressure Another pressure, which is perhaps the greatest cause of tension among teens today, is peer pressure. You are not alone in your desire to be accepted, liked, and thought of as successful. All people want to be liked, to have friends, and to win the affection and respect of others.

During high school, however, when young people are still trying to understand themselves, popularity seems to be especially important. Teens need to feel they are competing successfully for others' attention. With the close atmosphere of family receding and lifelong relationships of their own still in the future, young people need to belong to some group and know there is a special place where they are accepted. Somehow it is a sign to them that they are on the right track. The only problem, of course, is that teens must be selective about the people whose acceptance they seek. That's a big consideration, so check periodically to be sure your friends are on the right track themselves before you seek their advice.

The secret in handling peer pressure lies in understanding yourself and respecting your individuality. Many teens boast that they are independent, while actually they are some of the biggest followers around. They only wear what's in style; they listen only to "acceptable" music, and they only express attitudes others teens consider correct. That's not individuality. That's caving in to peer pressure.

Of course you will be expected to concede on occasion to please friends. Life is a give-and-take affair. Also, there will be times when you may decide to do what others want rather than insisting on your own preferences. The bottom line in dealing with peer pressure, though, is to promise yourself never to sell out on what is important to you.

Please the right person—you!

If your friends continually ask you to go against your own convictions, or pressure you into choices that are not comfortable for you, perhaps you and your "friends" are growing in two different directions. You may need to take another look at your relationships.

Peer pressure is no simple problem. No teen wants to be left out of the action or feel forced to spend evening after evening at home because he or she cannot make friends. The secret, as simple as it sounds, is in learning how to choose friends wisely in the first place and then remaining true to yourself while you are with them. If this happens, your friends will know and respect you. They will usually recognize your individuality when tempted to make you follow their lead.

If high school is a time for learning, which it certainly is, then one of the biggest lessons you can learn before that diploma is tucked under your arm is a solid faith in your own worth as a person. Peer pressure does not stop in adult life. It may become more subtle, but it is always there. If you can learn how to handle it and remain true to your good friends and your own convictions at the same time, you will be several giant steps ahead of many people.

Handling the big problems

If you can understand how to handle the pressure you feel from peers, you can also understand how to handle many other things. Sooner or later in your high school career, you will be invited to "party" with the gang. Depending on your area of the country, that may mean getting together to drink alcohol, or it may involve using marijuana and other drugs. The problem of alcohol and drugs in our society cannot be underestimated. It has ruined, and is ruining, many lives, and some of your friends may already be fighting their way out from under its spell.

Part of your high school education continues from junior high. It involves learning how to deal with drugs and alcohol in your own way and putting them into proper perspective. You may already be fighting your own battles with them, but if you can begin winning those battles, you are making a big step toward adulthood.

Go back to the bottom line

The secret to dealing with pressure to use drugs is to be your own person in any situation. If your insecurity prevents you from forming strong convictions of your own, it won't be easy to refuse that joint or pill, or to decide you would rather not get drunk. You will go along with the crowd.

Only you can make that final choice of which way to go. If you understand that artifical means of being happy are only temporary escapes from reality, you will know how to decide. If you realize that freedom from problems does not come from hiding them in a cloud of smoke, you will also understand that it is better and more honest to stick with your own strong convictions. While some people may call you a coward for not wanting to try drugs, the true coward is the person who cannot say "no" to the crowd.

The decision to use alcohol or other drugs is one of the roughest you will make during high school. It will also affect your later life considerably. Make that decision carefully. You owe that much to yourself.

Sex, dating, and peer pressure

Dating can bring on another tremendous pressure. Everything from magazine ads to the latest clothes and music reminds us we are living in a sex-conscious society. The macho image is prevalent in all commercials aimed at men. The sexy, appealing woman stares at us from an ad selling something as ordinary as toothpaste. This awareness of sex is everywhere; you cannot avoid it.

The emphasis on sex becomes evident to teens when a couple, after several dates, begins to start feeling the pressure to live up to the dating image. The boy feels he must have something suggestive or racy to say in the locker room on Monday. The girl often feels she has to go along with the guy's request on a date, or never have a date again. The pressure is tremendous.

This is another form of peer pressure, and it can be handled in the same way. Your date may tell others that things happened when they didn't. However, you and your partner know what really happened, and you must learn to be comfortable with that knowledge. There are few things in life that you *must* do. Freedom is the one thing every individual holds sacred. Our country was founded on an intense belief in it. Never let someone or some pressure for acceptance get in the way of your personal freedom and right to make your own choices.

You will make your life what you want it to be. You will choose to be who you want to be. Do yourself a favor. Base your decisions on a solid and truthful respect for yourself and your own personal integrity. The people who are important to you will understand. The others, by failing to accept the fact that you live your own life, will prove they really never have deserved your friendship.

Rapping It Up   Problems are a very real part of our lives. They may come from inside ourselves or from others. The secret to dealing with them is to face them honestly and understand what they are doing to us. Hiding from problems or trying to escape from them only brings on a whole new set of problems. Thus, life becomes even more complicated.

Your ability to handle the difficult situations will come directly from your own concept of yourself. If you know who you are and what you want, you can put each difficulty into its own perspective. You can make some intelligent choices.

Situations that already have gone wrong are in the past. Try to understand them, learn from them, and put them behind you. The problems of the present are simply challenges to your individuality. Face them. Analyze them. Then choose to deal with them from your own inner strength.

All people have problems. The truly great people, however, have learned how to cut their problems down to size by facing them squarely and taking action on them. How well you succeed in high school will be determined by who wins the battle—your problems or you. You can win that battle by using the ultimate secret weapon— yourself!

Points to Ponder   1. How much can you accept and appreciate your looks and your personality?

_____

_____

Do you feel any changes are necessary?

_____

What do you plan to do?

_____

_____

2. How much do you let your friends influence your decisions?

_____

Is this good or bad? _____ Why? _____

_____

_____

3. Who are the people who know the values and beliefs most important to you?

_____

4. How pressured do you feel to "do what is expected" when in a crowd or on a date?

_____

How can you rise above that pressure?

_____

_____

Coping with Crisis 16

"I've never made a mistake in my life, except once when I thought I had made one."

That's an old joke, and the humor of it lies in the fact that everyone does make mistakes. To think otherwise is foolish. But then, there are your mistakes! "Somehow everyone doesn't see my mistakes as a joke," you might say. "It seems I'm always doing something wrong. At least that's what people tell me!"

Others may tell you, sometimes in anger or disappointment, that you have failed. Failure is one thing, and you'll be reading about it. There is another, more intense feeling, though, and it comes when you know you've really done wrong! You know that sick, horrible feeling when you realize you've really "messed up," as the saying goes. These are the miserable times when you know you've disappointed someone or acted poorly when something really counted. No one can forget that frustrating feeling, that

119

emptiness and sense of anger at yourself. It hurts, knowing we may have hurt others. It bothers us, knowing we have done something, or failed to do something, that has affected others or their opinion and trust in us.

Mistakes, the feeling of failure, and the depression that is sure to come are hard to take. While you're in your teens, these feelings can be even more devastating. You're at a stage when report cards keep reminding you of your success or lack of it. Every grading period at school you see in black and white where you have failed, or have not accomplished your best. Parents, teachers, and employers are all authority figures, and because they have power over you, they feel it is their right and obligation to let you know where you are going wrong. In fact, sometimes they aren't very gentle about it!

After a few mistakes on your part, you naturally become a bit more cautious. You pull back. You may even start to feel paranoid—suspicious, fearful, and on the lookout for the next time someone will catch you doing wrong. Soon you begin to feel the tension of always being on the defensive.

It is that fear of doing wrong, in fact, that often keeps you from trying. After you've experienced a few colossal failures, you may be tempted to play it safe, do as little as possible, and stay at least partially successful. However, the fact remains that the only people who never do anything wrong are the people who never do anything!

Everyone Does It   The first thing to remember whenever you get that sick feeling of failure is that you are not alone. It's just another way life has of letting you know you're a member of the human race. You will make mistakes. How you understand and use your mistakes, however, will affect the quality of your life, the stability of your emotions, and the amount of happiness you can achieve.

Recall the things you've learned so far about your own personality. How positive can you be? How excited can you get about the possibility of things improving? How fast can you bounce back from hard times? How do you deal with failure? Do you blame others? Do you keep it all inside and give yourself forty mental lashes, or do you share it with someone, clearing the air and putting it behind you?

Failure is part of life. How you handle it will determine whether you're able to learn from your errors and move on with your life. You're going to make mistakes, but the true test is whether failure destroys your self-confidence or makes you more determined to change things for the better—even in spite of yourself!

The next time you fail, look at what happened. Where did the failure occur? Was it in yourself, or was it someone else whose rejection made you feel like a failure? Was it a failed test, not being chosen for a team or a school play, or breaking a rule at home or at school?

The Biggest Disappointment of All

Probably the hardest failure to deal with, just because it is so intense, is the failure you feel as a person. The disappointment when you have let someone down, or when you've hurt someone you care about, is the worst.

Beth, for example, had been told a confidential secret by one of her dearest friends. The friend had gotten into a serious situation and wanted it kept private. To ease her anxiety, though, she shared the problem with Beth. Beth knew it was serious and could hurt her friend's reputation if word got around. However, at lunch one day Beth put her mouth into operation before her brain was in gear. She let part of the secret slip out.

Once she said the words, Beth knew she had betrayed a confidence, and that horrible feeling came over her. When the others asked for more information, she knew she had already said too much, and she tried to back down on the story. But she had said enough, and the damage was done.

That feeling of knowing you failed miserably when someone trusted you can be shattering. You know you're a better person than that. You know you can be trusted and that you care. You know it—and at times you also know you can lose it all and fail as a friend and a person. What can you do?

It happens. Realize that. Be sorry for your mistakes, and let that sinking feeling hold your attention a while. This may sound a bit strange, but sometimes the best way to learn is by getting things wrong. Missing a question on a test may make you remember that information more clearly than if you had gotten it right the first time. That little feeling of anger at yourself makes a strong impression on your mind. The next time you see that question, it will be much easier to answer.

The same thing holds true for mistakes you make as a person. The only way to learn to be a sincere, honest person is by being one. Part of the territory of living is the possibility, and the probability, that you will make some mistakes. When they happen, face up to them, and then see what you have learned.

Now that Beth has betrayed her friend, she has a few choices. She can lie about it and say someone else must have leaked out the news. She can be cold, saying the other girl is expecting too much, and defend herself. But the best thing, and the only honest thing, is to let her friend know she told the secret (without meaning to), and that she is sorry. Few personal failures are intentional. Beth didn't want to hurt her friend. It just happened.

Others can talk about rules and living perfectly all they want. You know there will be times when you do something unworthy. The reason may be that you just let it happen. You are not perfect, and neither is anyone else. You have faults; so does everyone else. But you are basically good, and certainly so is everyone else!

When your mistake is a big one, it will make an impression on you. If you remember that feeling, you may keep yourself from making the same mistake again. If you want to be a better person, you can use all those errors to definite advantage. Then you'll know to be more careful next time, and you won't make the same mistake again. Beth realized she often said whatever came to her mind without thinking of the consequences. Once she admitted this to herself, she began to think twice before speaking. You can learn the same kind of lesson.

Making the Same Mistake Twice

You may not learn from a mistake the first time you make it. If we all learned from our mistakes as they happened, everyone would reach perfection around age 25 or 26. You may have realized from some adults that this isn't the case! It never will be. You may do something wrong and, weeks or months later, make the same mistake again. This, too, just proves you are normal. When you repeat a mistake, go back and check your list of values and priorities. If something is important to you, you probably will learn it the first time and move on. If it isn't important, that impression won't be as strong. When the temptation presents itself again, you may fail again.

You will have to determine what is important. Do you want to be a good friend? Do you want others to think of you as someone they can trust? If you answer "yes," you'll learn how to keep your friends' confidences to yourself. You are responsible when it comes to your failing, just as you are responsible for every other part of your life. If you want to succeed, you will. If you can learn that one mistake isn't going to ruin you, you'll make it.

Just look inside yourself. Is the problem in your personality? Is it caused by a hot temper or a lack of confidence? Once you see the reasons behind these problems you seem to be having, you should be able to find some ways of solving them and making fewer mistakes in the future.

People Problems

Then there are other people. You can't control them. You can't always please them, and you definitely can't always be aware of how they will react to you or your decisions. Failure that comes to us from others is always hard to take. It's especially hard if they are people we care about.

Rejection, for example, is one of the hardest things. You may want someone, or some group, to accept you. You do your best. You really try, and still you are rejected. They just don't seem to want you, and that hurts. What can you do? You can look at possible reasons. There may be a flaw in your personality, and there may not be. Those others may just not be your kind of people. They may be too busy in their own worlds to discover how interesting and pleasant it is to be with you. That's their problem. It may hurt for a while, but don't let it be your problem.

When you fail with people who are already a part of your life, you'll have to learn some hard facts, too. Your parents, for example, will let you know when you've let them down. They may even tell you how disappointed they are, and that can really get to you.

Consider this girl's situation: "I remember one night, after we had a horrible fight. I was really angry, and I said a lot of things I probably didn't mean. But I was mad, and I wanted my parents to know it. Later, I walked into the kitchen and saw my mother sitting at the table. She was crying. She just looked at me, and I wanted to die. I do love her, but she had made me so mad. I felt so confused and so mad. I was mad at myself for hurting her and still mad at her for what she had done. Talk about confusion."

When you hurt the people you love, it is not easy to get over the experience. You can try to understand it later, when you are in a calmer state of mind. Often that will be the best thing to do. Just remembering how you felt is the first step. In this girl's case, those tears in her mother's eyes can teach more lessons than any lecture or textbook.

Parents and Teachers   There will be times when family members will affect you. For example, a parent going through a divorce can often try to turn children against the marriage partner who is leaving. This not only tears up everyone's feelings. It can also give terrible guilt feelings to the sons and daughters. Or, in another type of case, some parents make their children feel guilty every time they do wrong. "I really am a rotten parent," they'll say. "I tried so hard, and now you act like this. Where did I go wrong?"

Feeling like a failure usually includes a feeling of guilt. You'll get enough of it on your own throughout your life. You don't need any more. If your folks have the habit of making you feel guilty, try talking to them about it. Don't let yourself feel guilty all the time. There's no future in it.

Family conflict is always rough. When someone outside the home says you have failed, you can at least go home and forget it. When the people you live with do it, you'll have to get some honest communication going, or the problem will only get worse.

Teachers may also make you feel you have failed. Failure that appears on a report card or through a talk with a teacher also is hard to face. However, most often these feelings can be eased by speaking frankly about yourself. If you can get the teacher to see you as a person with individual needs and frustrations, he or she will probably listen. That doesn't mean that your test scores won't affect your grade. But if the teacher understands a bit more about you, he or she may make more of an effort to help you do well in the course.

What's the best way to deal with your failures with others? Talk to them. Explain. Defend without being defensive. Listen without judging. Usually, once emotional differences have been discussed, a lot more understanding will flow between you and those problem people. From there, the road to success will have fewer bumps.

I Can't Do Anything Right!   Never label yourself as a failure. So, you didn't get an A on that last test, and you weren't chosen to be in the play. Maybe your story wasn't chosen as one of the best in the class, and you don't seem to do anything well enough to please your math teacher. All those things that make you feel like a failure are just single items. True, you may not be a genius, and you may have two left feet. But everyone around you has their weaknesses, too.

Failing at one thing doesn't mean you are a failure at

everything. Most people who let their failures affect them are individuals who can't work up the courage to try again. Do try! Find the things you're good at, and move on. All kinds of skills and abilities can give you the success you need. You may find a clue to your true talents in some item announced in the next school bulletin, or hidden in a conversation you'll soon have with a new friend. Your abilities are there, just begging for you to discover them. Give it a try!

Rapping It Up   Failure is something that will always be lurking somewhere in your life. It will come from you, or from things and people around you. What can you do about it? You can learn not to fear it, and you can begin to make failure work *for* you, not against you. By letting it sink in, understanding the reason for it, and then deciding to go on, you can see to it that failures don't ruin your life, but instead make it more open and honest. There is no shame in failing, and there is no shame in admitting it. In fact, it may be one of the healthiest things you can do.

The only shame lies in wallowing in your own defeat and deciding not to go on. The failure lies in blaming others. If you can keep loving yourself, the people around you, and the things that are important to you, you're bound to succeed eventually. The only real failure is not loving, not caring, and not believing enough in yourself to know you can succeed. Look back at the dedication in this book. Is this book dedicated to you? If it isn't right now, improving your attitude could change that!

Points to Ponder   1. What kinds of failures do you fear most?

_____

_____

Why?

_____

_____

2. Which of your personality traits cause most of your failures? Explain with an example.

_____

_____

_____

_____

3. How often do you let feelings of guilt linger?

_____

What do you do to get rid of them?

_____

_____

4. Give an example of one instance when you learned from a mistake.

_____

_____

_____

5. What advice would you give a friend who feels there is no use in trying again after a rejection or a failure?

_____

_____

Beating the Raps 17

Guaranteed. The hardest chapter to read in this book.

Guaranteed. Some words to make you think, and possibly make you angry.

Guaranteed. Some of the best words you can read at this time of your life.

No book on succeeding in high school would be fair to you, or complete, without letting you know what others think of your generation. While every teen generation is talked about by the adult world, something different seems to be happening lately. Many people—from teachers to businesspeople to parents and psychologists—have the same thoughts these days. The consensus is that something has been happening to young people, and whatever it is, it is not good.

We're talking about a *rap* here, not in the style of M.C. Hammer, but in the sense of harsh blame. And there are a few raps against people your age that seem to be heard whenever adults who deal with teens get together. They are spoken with a sense of worry and concern, and you should be aware of them. Why are these adults so concerned? They know that you, and people your age, will take over the management of this country and this world, and they are puzzled by what they see, and what they don't see, in your generation.

In the next few pages, we'll go over some of the biggest raps. You may find yourself in them, or you may be angry about them because they are not true in your case. That will be good. In any case, here are the problems some people see in your age group these days. Read them, and if they ring true, determine to make some changes so that they don't apply to you in the future.

"Teens Today Just Don't Care"

This is the first bad rap against your generation. It comes from people who have teens working for them, from teachers to coaches, and from other adults. In every era, of course, teens have much to learn. They're so busy sorting out their own lives that most of them don't get too involved in the news, in broader areas of knowledge, or in keeping up with current thinking and attitudes. That has always been the case.

Some feel today's teens show an attitude that goes even further. Many in your age group not only don't know, but they don't seem to *care* that they don't know. That's a big difference. You do know many things. You've known at least a quick war—in the Persian Gulf. You've seen the reports of death, injury, and even atrocities committed against other human beings. You know how the world reacts to many things.

But do you form your own opinions about these world events? Do you take time to analyze them and stay informed about them? An important step in growing up is learning to care about things outside yourself. Being a mature adult means giving up the self-absorption that's natural in children. As an adult, you are not only a responsible member of your own family, but an important member of your community and of the world.

That's a big responsibility. How do you handle it? Try to keep your mind open to new ideas and opinions. Read a newspaper once in a while. Turn off the cable music channel long enough to learn what's going on in the world. Let yourself be open to events and concerns the world is sharing. And, when you're old enough, register to vote.

Another step is to *want* education, rather than viewing it as something that is inflicted on you merely because of your age and society's laws. Education is a privilege of free societies. Value yours.

"They're So Selfish!" The second big rap involves a feeling that your age group is very selfish. Many adults feel you don't care about anything except your own pleasure. If it isn't "fun" for you, you don't want any part of it. You seem to be very materialistic, expecting rewards for anything you do, even if your work and effort are only mediocre. From payment to report cards to demanding good grades at school or more spending money on the home front, many teens are creating the impression that they don't know how to give. They are only interested in taking.

Also, a great many young people become involved with drugs or alcohol. Others develop casual attitudes about sexual involvement. Adults see these problems as an indication that many teens are selfish and desire only their own pleasure.

How can you respond to these charges? Prove people wrong by your actions. When needs arise in your school, community, or family, show your concern. Turn away from the mirror every now and then and see where you can help. Get in the giving mode. And develop a personal code of ethics that shows a healthy respect for others as well as yourself.

"They Have No Motivation" Many adults feel most teens have no real motivation and no follow-through on projects. "It's as if the last burner isn't on with these kids," some would say. "They seem to be in some kind of fog, and they don't mind being in it. They can't be counted on to follow through on projects, and they don't place any value on membership in anything— from a family to a team or group."

Those who sponsor extracurricular activities at schools echo this sentiment. From the teacher who has to take over preparations for a fund raiser to another who has to finish the work her staff members or theater group didn't get done, many feel this is the wrong time to be involved with activities where student participation is involved. Sponsors say, "Students start out and talk about their plans a long time. But then they fall behind far from the finish line, or they do work that is so poor it can't be used."

If you think there's a teacher or coach who feels this way about you, what's the answer? In the words of one coach, "Get with it!" Show adults in your life that you can be responsible. Prove you do have a desire to make things happen. Get involved not for the glory or for another picture in the school yearbook, but because you have something to give to your extracurricular groups. And then give!

"They Just Don't Want to Work"

The third rap is a charge of laziness and acceptance of mediocrity. Many local employers feel teens aren't worth hiring because they do the least work and then expect pay much higher than they deserve. The big rap is that teens tend to accept mediocrity as the norm and that they have little desire to give a solid effort to any project.

Some schools have watered down their grading systems; yours may be one of them. When your parents went to school 70 percent was a passing grade, and 69 percent was a failure. One had to achieve 95 percent or higher to get an A. In some schools now, grading levels have been lowered by ten points, and anything higher than 90 percent is called an A.

Yet when teachers give percentage grades or letter grades, many feel students demand higher marks for mediocre work. "It's as if we've lowered all our standards and norms for real excellence," one teacher said recently. "Students do half-baked work and then are angry when they don't get the highest grades."

You may need to realize that merely doing a project is only half the battle. Doing it well is the other half. Writing a paper and handing in the first draft is not usually worth a good grade. If this is your mode of operation, don't expect the highest mark for mediocre effort. Most papers need to be revised more than once.

How can you beat this rap? Work. Take time to relax and enjoy your friends. Listen to your music. But when work needs to be done, do it. Remember that section on work ethic in an earlier chapter? Review it if you need to. Show people you know how to make an honest effort, that you understand commitment to a job and a desire to do something worthwhile.

Don't be like the teenager who sat listening to his stereo while his mother raked all the leaves in the yard, then told his neighbor she'd better get working in her own yard. Let others know you are willing to be part of the work ethic which has built your country and brought it to the present time. Let adults know you are willing to add your own effort to making it even better in years to come. How? By showing a willingness to work hard and honestly now. Be part of the work at home. Be part of the work at school. Be part of society's work today.

"They Can't Think for Themselves"

Because of teens' tendency to follow the crowd, which often leads to heavy drinking, drugs, and other things, adults also say you are a bunch of sheep. Whether it's belonging to a gang in some areas, or hanging onto a clique, many teens seem to give in to herd-mentality thinking.

You've been accused of having little creativity and independence. You've been accused of being used by everyone from drug dealers to some of your own pseudointellectual leaders. In a very sad new phenomenon, adults are also seeing a rise in racism and hatred coming from your generation. Whether it is hatred of cultures or minorities, or more subtle forms of hatred, there is a part of your generation that seems to think hating is "in," and that it's all right to be cruel to others who are not like you.

That may be the most dire concern about your generation. Most adults hope we're moving beyond the hatred of earlier times. To see young people take up the banner of hatred again is to feel that the world is not improving and, worse, that we're possibly regressing to earlier mistakes and stupidities.

"They Can't Accept Responsibility"

Another rap you can really do something about is the belief adults have that you can't accept responsibility for your actions or words. Parents, teachers, and employers are quick to bring out examples of teens' inability to take the responsibility or the blame for anything. "The student blamed me for his bad grade. Yet it was his low test scores which added up to that final mark. His answer is that I don't like him. That's why he got the low grade."

One parent had this to say: "My daughter can never admit she did anything wrong. It's always someone else's fault. She can never simply say she made a mistake. She's so quick to defend herself; she seems unable to admit she can make mistakes. Halfway through any sentence when I'm telling her what went wrong, she's already interrupting with an excuse that puts all the blame on someone or something else! Why can't she realize that some things *are* her fault?"

What's the answer? Easy. No one expects you to be perfect. No one expects you to be right all the time and never make mistakes. No one expects you to achieve your best all the time. We all have bad days. Just admit when you do have them. Admit you didn't handle a project well. Admit you made a mistake. It's the adult thing to do.

Rapping It Up   By this time you may be ready to burn this book. Instead, give it to someone else to read, and start a new fire inside yourself. Now that you know what some adults think about your age group, be determined to show that you don't fit that negative description.

Care. Care about the world around you and the world in which you live. Care about your family members and friends. Care about your own ability to live responsibly and productively in the adult world. Don't be afraid to go out of your way to show concern for others. Try to overcome selfishness when you're tempted into it, and try to show you desire to know what the world is thinking and feeling. Get in the giving and caring mode.

If you want the respect of others and expect them to begin treating you like an adult, start accepting and acknowledging responsibility. Listen to others' criticism of your work, then consider their words and make a reasonable response. It is the child who always puts the blame elsewhere. Constantly fighting off blame doesn't give others the idea you have moved much beyond childhood.

Show some motivation at home, in school, in the community, and in your life. Finish the projects you start, and decide to make a valid contribution to the groups in which you hold membership. Rather than expect favors or fight about grades, produce. Show others you're not afraid of hard work and that you have the ability to see things through with the best effort you can give.

So much for the raps. Now the world awaits your response.

Points to Ponder   1. Name something you could do this week to become better informed about current events.

_____

2. What was the last generous thing you did for someone in your family? Name something else you could do to show your parents or brothers and sisters that you care.

   _____

   _____

   _____

3. Are you in the middle of any extracurricular or class projects?

   _____

   How do you plan to complete the work on time?

   _____

   _____

4. How strong is your work ethic? _____ What could you do to improve your work at home, in school, or at your part-time job?

   _____

   _____

   _____

5. How much do others influence your opinions and actions? Explain.

   _____

   _____

   _____

6. Are you able to admit when you've made a mistake? Explain with an example.

   _____

   _____

   _____

Free at Last! 18

Every country values it. Many nations fight wars for it. Yet as you begin to claim it, the only battle will be in your own head.

Independence. It's on the way, and you're the one who will determine how soon you achieve it, based on what you do and think now.

Nothing Succeeds like Success

Teenagers need more independence and freedom as they progress through high school. Yet, too many parents fear the worst and, as a result, keep their sons and daughters at home under tight rules, with severe restrictions on their social lives. Success only comes from other successes you have had. And success is impossible without the freedom to try. Your folks will have to understand that you may need some room for growing, and for making a few mistakes.

You can help them understand this by showing them a few signs that you deserve their trust. And keep your mistakes to a bare minimum.

Remember that most adults aren't expecting you to handle all situations with a lot of maturity and responsibility. You may be insulted at this little piece of information, but the law—the legal system—considers you immature. That's why all those rules for minors exist.

Many adults may have their doubts about your ability to succeed. However, if you can surprise them every chance you get, you should be able to make them notice you are changing. Instead of showing negative reactions around the house—like pouting, complaining, or trying to get out of all the work you can—do the reverse. You may leave a few mouths open in astonishment, but as you begin carrying your weight at home and acting like a positive force in your family, the message is sure to get through!

The same approach applies at school. Teachers are used to complaints whenever homework or a test is announced. They're just waiting for a few groans and negative comments. They're braced for them. How about giving them a shock? Keep those remarks unsaid a time or two. You'll catch your teachers off guard, and they'll begin to wonder if you really are that "kid" they thought you were, or if you are on the way toward becoming a more positive and realistic individual.

There is one more person you have to convince that you are not a kid anymore—yourself. You will never be able to convince anyone else that you are growing and becoming more responsible unless you believe it first. Go back to all those successes you've had. Make sure you stay aware of them. They'll give you the confidence to be more sure of yourself the next time you must move into action. They'll also help you realize that your childhood is a thing of the past.

Try to leave your negative attitude behind, and begin to believe you have something worthwhile to offer others. You can be trusted with their secrets and property. You can handle situations that demand maturity and good sense. You can be counted on! Once you believe in yourself, that belief will radiate to others. Your own confidence in yourself will make others more confident in you. If you act like a champ, you will be a champ. If you act like a chump, don't blame others for thinking you are one.

A Winning Combination

Independence. Maturity. Responsibility. These can be scary words. However, if you can put these three qualities together, you'll be able to get all the freedom you need.

You deserve to be thought of as a capable person. You deserve respect. You deserve recognition for your abilities. Show a bit of those three characteristics, and you'll get what you need and deserve.

"If I show my parents some independence around the house, they'll kill me," you might say. Maybe. One of the best places to begin to act independently is with your own friends, not at home. Your folks may need to see you handle independence before they start loosening the ties. Let them see it by starting with the people in your group.

Bob enjoys the outdoors. He really enjoys hiking and camping. Over a long weekend, he may have the chance to go camping, and he may want to go.

"You're kidding," his pals might say. "Take off to the woods and eat with the mosquitoes when you could be at the concert downtown? You're out of your mind!"

Bob has two choices, right? He may not be interested in music and may have no trouble knowing what he wants to do. His parents know his options, too. They wait and watch. Will Bob have the independence to do what he wants, or will he give in to peer pressure and go along with the crowd? Sure, he'll have a good time at the concert, but he'd rather be camping. Who cares about a few mosquitoes or chiggers?

If Bob does what he wants, which in this case isn't hurting anyone, he can prove to himself and to those around him that he is his own person. His friends will survive without his company at the concert, and his folks will begin to understand that Bob doesn't always follow the crowd. He's showing some good, strong personal independence. By making his own decision, and being comfortable and confident in it, Bob can take some giant steps toward independent living. Another way you can show independence is by letting people see some leadership. "Me?" you might say. "I don't know if I can do it. And besides, when can I get a chance?"

You may baby-sit. You have friends over to the house, and you are involved in different activities. Showing some spunk once in a while and suggesting new ideas can help. If you always follow and never show desire to take the initiative, others won't think you have any sense of independence. There are ways of showing that you have a mind of your own without turning people off. You can suggest things without demanding and take charge without becoming a dictator.

Independence is won, not necessarily given. Once you prove yourself, you will gain the freedom you want. Give it a try.

Maturity Is a Busy Word!

Maturity doesn't come with age or authority. It is simply using the common sense you have in a responsible way. Acting and reacting with calm, honest sincerity, you can achieve maturity just by being aware of your own worth and the worth of people you meet. That knowledge will give you the confidence to be the leader in major decisions, to listen sincerely to others, and to take on responsibilities that come your way.

Rapping It Up

You do deserve the freedom you want. You have a right to it, and, in your own time, you will get it. The way to obtain freedom is by earning the right to it. By showing some self-assurance, some leadership and independent thinking, and by handling the situations that come along responsibly, you will show people you are ready for even more independence.

There are many characteristics the adult person shows. If you begin to give some hints of them, others will notice you are moving well beyond the "kid" stage. One of those key characteristics is an ability to forget about yourself once in a while and think of others. Sure, we all think first of ourselves; that's only normal. When people give you their best, however, it would be a sign of maturity for you to show some appreciation. Recognizing the goodness and effort of others is evidence of the growing adult in you. You prove by saying "thank you" that you are not just out for all you can get. Only children believe the world revolves around them—that everyone owes them what they want. The adult has learned the foolishness of such a silly idea. By acknowledging the things people have done for you, you show you are man or woman enough to be aware of their feelings, too. Your friends and the adults in your life who go out of their way for you may often feel unappreciated and forgotten. It's so easy to take people for granted. "That's just part of their job," you might say. But giving genuine concern is never part of a job. It is a sign of unselfish human greatness. Your parents, teachers, and friends have feelings, too. They need some positive reaction once in a while. Make sure those in your life know that you think of them as more than simply people who can give you what you want.

Unselfishness and awareness of others will develop mature qualities in you. By being grateful and stepping into another's shoes once in a while, you can show you are more than a taker. Maturity means knowing how to give. Give others the gift of your sincerity, responsibility, and gratitude. The gift comes back, always. In fact, it comes back with a greater acknowledgment that you are nearing adulthood.

No one wants to keep you from growing up. Rather, many people are waiting to see those first signs that show you are on your way. They're waiting for them as they wait for the first spring flowers. Give them those signs, and you'll notice the difference in their reactions.

The giver always receives.

The person who can say a genuine "thank you" is not only mature, but capable of greatness.

Points to Ponder

1. How often do you actually talk in a calm way to the adults in your life, expressing your need for freedom?

   _____

   How could you do this more effectively?

   _____

   _____

2. In what area of your life have you matured most during the last year? Be specific and give an example.

   _____

   _____

   _____

3. Which of your characteristics prevent you from acting more maturely?

   _____

   _____

   How does this happen?

   _____

   _____

4. In what ways can you improve your sense of responsibility?

_____

_____

Who could help you most in this regard, and how?

_____

_____

Turn Your Dreams into Goals

19

There's one good thing anyone can say for high school. No matter how grim some days might be or how much pressure, disappointment, or tension you feel—it ends.

"Hurray!" A first- or second-year student will say, "And it won't end one day too soon for me!" A junior may take a little more time to come up with that remark. A senior may say it, but there may be a strange lump somewhere deep in the throat. Why?

High school has its own set of problems, and you have taken a good look at them in this book. There is another dimension of high school, however, that always remains somewhere in the background. It's that sure feeling that whatever is going on now won't last. High school is just a stepping-stone that leads to a long and demanding future. As difficult as high school may seem sometimes, at least you become familiar with it. You know what others expect of you, and the routine becomes familiar, and things get easier.

The future is uncertain. It always is. No matter how bad things seem for you now, there is always a feeling of security. At least you know what's going on, even if you may not like it. Yet the future is another story. What will you do when you finally get that precious diploma? How will you leave all the friends you've made, and how can you be sure there will be new friends to take their place? Pressures caused by high school tend to ease up as you get into the routine and learn to cope. The extra pressure of high school, however, is knowing that it will end. Then what will you do?

Cliff Hangers

"I feel like I'm getting ready to jump off a cliff," one senior remarked a few months before graduation. "I've come to the end of the land, and now there's nothing ahead of me but a bunch of clouds and a lot of nothingness. I can't see what's out there, and it's scary." Sure, it's scary. Moving on is never easy because you can never be sure of what you will find. Even if what has gone before hasn't been that great, at least you knew it, and you could deal with it.

Some teens, on the other hand, look toward the future as an escape. "I can't wait to get out of the house and off on my own. I can't wait to get all these teachers behind me and start doing things my way!" Sounds good. One little nagging attitude seems to creep into these remarks, though, and it makes them sound hollow. Remarks such as these are made by teens who feel no satisfaction, happiness, or success in their past or present condition. They think the future is where they will finally be happy, rich, with a great job—if they need a job at all.

A little hint, though. The future is built on the past, and happiness grows over the years, if it is going to grow at all. True, there should be better years ahead, full of deeper love, richer happiness, and greater satisfaction. That's the way it should be. If leaving high school seems a way of getting out of the house, walking away from authority, and running off to live your own life just the way you want it to be, though, there are be a few big mistakes in your thinking. You will leave home soon enough. Don't leave it on a sour note.

The future isn't an escape. It can't be, because you are taking one big part of the past into it—yourself! Take a little time to realize this. Understand that you don't solve anything by moving away, but only by moving toward something greater and better. How solidly good and rewarding your future will be depends on what you can bring to it from the past—from the *you* that has been.

Your future is up there, all right. It shouldn't be scary because you have built within that terrific self of yours, that strong, unbeatable will to survive and succeed. Grab hold of it, and don't run away to the future. Run into it with all the goodness and love and determination that have been in your life so far. If you can't see that goodness, take another look. It's there. It will make the difference between the future being a repetition of the past or an exciting time where the thrill of challenge and the search for success make every day unique and full of hope.

What Would You Say? Write some short pieces of advice to students who view the future in the following ways.

1. Kristen has lived in a broken home for years. There are a lot of problems there, but now she has a boyfriend who really cares about her. He doesn't have a good job yet, and Kristen hasn't really decided what she wants to do as a career. But life is so miserable at home that she is considering marriage. At least it would make life better, she says.

   _____

   _____

   _____

2. Steve doesn't think college is the answer. He has a chance to work at a local business, and he feels he will be able to advance in this business without a college degree. What would you tell him?

   _____

   _____

   _____

   _____

3. Scott and Julie both want successful careers, but they can't find a university that would offer equally good programs for both of them. Should one give up the chance to get a degree at the best university so that they can go to the same school and keep seeing each other?

_____

_____

_____

_____

4. Cindy hasn't been very happy in high school. She really doesn't want to go to college, but she's going to have to do something after graduation. She thinks maybe she'll just keep living at home, get a job as a waitress, and see what happens.

_____

_____

_____

_____

_____

Your Turn   In this space, or on a separate piece of paper, answer these two questions.

1. What do you see yourself doing twenty years from now? Describe your future.

_____

_____

_____

_____

_____

2. How will you make these things happen?

_____

_____

_____

_____

_____

_____

Where's the Goal Line?   Thinking about the future means setting a few goals and making some plans and decisions. Remember, you don't have to plan your whole life during these four years, but it is wise to begin some serious thinking.

Of course, your counselor, your folks, a favorite teacher, or even your friends may help you consider the future. But as you start thinking of an answer to the question, "What do I want to be?" first of all, resolve to *be yourself!* Don't fall into the delusion of choosing a career for any other reason than that you will feel fulfilled doing it. Too many young adults go into careers for the money, the prestige, or because they feel it is the "career of today." They may end up miserable—stuck in careers that are not comfortable for them. And they may not have enough courage to leave that first line of work and go into something they feel would really be right for them.

If you are a first- or second-year student, you may have no desire to plan on college at the present. Keep your options open, however, since you may change your mind before you graduate. If you are a junior or senior, the pressure may seem much more real. At least you can take college entrance tests to find out where you might fit in on the campus scene. You may have underestimated your own ability, and once you realize you are capable of more than you had guessed, you can get the courage to choose a more challenging and satisfying career.

Girls who think they will get married soon after high school and live within a family structure of their own may need to look at some statistics. Four out of every five women eventually live without a marriage partner because of death, divorce, or choosing the single life. If you don't plan a career now, you will probably regret it later. You don't want to run the risk of eventually entering a tight job market with no skills or experience. Think about it. A little training never hurts, and in the long run it is you who must decide not to be hurt by poor planning while you are young.

It is also true that many married women hold jobs in today's society. Prices keep rising, and many families need two incomes to keep up with the cost of living. And many women enjoy their careers and make them a high priority throughout their lives. So although developing a skill or profession may seem unnecessary to you, it is crucial. Making preparations now to be able to handle a good job later is never foolish.

Your goals may be unclear now, but they should be made with a calm and realistic eye to the future. Check out your abilities and potential with your counselor, then consider your choices. Leave the daydreams aside, and make your dreams goals. A dream is wishful thinking. A goal is something you can reach with planning. Plan. Set some goals for your immediate future after high school. Then give yourself the luxury of more distant goals, too. Life will change. However, if you can at least set yourself in the right direction, you can handle those changes up ahead with confidence in yourself and your abilities.

Career Goals

The secret to planning for the future lies in being able to handle pressure. Your parents may try to design your future down to the last detail. Don't let them do it. True, they may want you to be a success. Every parent does. They cannot plan your life for you, though, because they cannot live your life. Help them realize you are your own person, but also seek their advice. They have had a few more years and experience, and their wisdom can help. You, however, should be expected to make the final decisions when it comes to school and career. If your parents make them for you now, you'll never feel you had a chance to begin in a way that was right for you.

Your folks may measure you against older brothers and sisters. If your older brother got a full-time job at 18, you shouldn't feel pressured to do the same. If your older sister is in med school, that's great. However, you shouldn't feel it is your duty to follow her there. Maturity means being able to make responsible decisions, remember? Get all the help you can. Then take an honest look at yourself. Set your goals high, but be realistic, and choose to set yourself on a path that will be comfortable yet challenging for you.

The biggest pressure you feel concerning the future may come from inside yourself. How badly do you want success? How about money, prestige, and love? Do you feel you must choose a career that pays the highest salary? Or can you be smart enough to aim for a profession that may not be the most impressive, but that is right for you?

If you like people, for example, don't bottle yourself up in a profession where contact with others will be limited. You may make good money, but you'll also probably be frustrated after a short time. If you have a hard time dealing with pressure and work yourself into a frenzy until every little thing is perfect, don't choose a career where you will be wrapped up with details for the rest of your life. The more you understand yourself, the greater will be your chance of selecting a profession where you will feel successful, happy, and at peace with yourself.

Where Do I Go from Here?

Life will go on after high school, and the transition won't be as traumatic as you might think. One by one, the puzzle pieces of that first year or two after graduation will fall into place, and you'll begin to see yourself changing. One of the first choices that will help you get a solid feeling about your future will be your decision about school. Once you know if and where you are going, getting there doesn't seem quite so frightening.

"Great! So where do I go?" There may be a few people who are just dying to give you an answer to that one, but right now, they don't matter. *You* matter, and as you try to come to a decision about the future, don't rule out the possibility of more education.

The decision may seem absolutely agonizing right now, but it really isn't. College is not as regimented as high school, and neither are the many trade schools available to young men and women. If you don't want to think about college, check into those schools that teach skills you are interested in developing. The armed forces are another option. Almost every profession has some training school for future members, and if you need some help finding one, talk to your counselor. If you choose to forget about college, don't also choose to stop your education right after high school. There is just too much at stake—your life!

The lure of a supposedly high-paying job now may tempt you. However, if that job holds no chance for promotion or expansion of your talents, it will be a dead end in a few years. A good check may look great to a high school graduate, but it can never replace the long-term value of challenge and preparation for the rest of your life. The world is getting more and more competitive. Few opportunities are available to those who have ended their education with a high school diploma. The world has changed since your parents were in school; further education is something almost everyone should consider.

If you think college is a possibility, there are some steps you'll need to take to narrow down your choice. Living on campus used to be a must, but now the many junior colleges and local schools provide the option of living at home. You can work part-time while still earning your degree. Local colleges may not offer the expansive sports activities or sprawling campuses of bigger schools, but they are well-equipped to handle many career preparations. And they are usually less expensive, which is nothing to be overlooked.

"No, I need to get off on my own," you might say. Or you may have decided on a career already and know the best-equipped place to handle your specific needs is a university. In that case, your state universities will be the easiest to get into, and they will also be the cheapest. Private schools tend to cost more, but if you want to attend one of them, they offer a smaller campus and the closeness that is not easily obtained at a large university.

Going away for college will give you the opportunity to begin life on your own. It is the first big break from family life, and it will give you a chance to see how well you can decide, manage, and survive without your parents watching every move. At first, all that freedom may be a bit much for you to handle, but it will show you who you really are. It may also help you decide if you want to stay that way, or perhaps mature more.

What School Is Right for Me?

"All I know is that I want a prestige school," a student once said. At first, that comment sounds a bit unreal, but this girl wanted to enter a highly competitive career. She knew if she attended one of the premier schools in her field, her chances of working her way to the top were better, and her reasoning was correct.

If your parents can afford it, and if you know one particular school can give you what you need, go to it. Just make sure you have enough valid reasons for choosing a school where the tuition may be as high as the center on the basketball team. Your parents want the best for you, but you also have the obligation of choosing what is reasonable for them. There are always scholarships and grants, too. Check into these. Many of them go unused year after year just because students who could have benefited from them were unaware of them or were too lazy to do the necessary paperwork to get the money. Once again, this is a place where your counselor can be a big help.

Another temptation you might have to fight is the lure of going to a "party" school where a number of your friends may be enrolling. True, there are many good times at any college. The pressure of study and deadlines must be relieved in some way. There are schools everywhere, however, that sometimes become havens for young "adults" who are not really serious about their futures. The tendency, once many of these people get together, is to forget the books and have fun. "Why bother doing today what we can put off until tomorrow?" seems to sum up their attitude toward study.

Some teens find themselves in a real dilemma when they face this situation. They know they have to keep up with their studies, yet they are easily drawn to a party down the hall, or to an event they know will keep them up late and ruin their ability to concentrate the next day. Part of going away to school, remember, is learning how to make your own decisions. The college you choose may be a "party" school, but wherever you go, you'll eventually have to learn how to cope with pressures put on you by others, and how to schedule your time.

Is Marriage for Me?

Marriage is a lifetime commitment. At least that's what it's supposed to be. How far away is it for you? How much do you want it?

Another big pressure put on teens after they graduate from high school is others urging them to date and eventually marry. If you intend to stay free for a career, or just feel you need more time before you give yourself to someone who is worth your love and the rest of your life, you'll have to face these decisions realistically. It is possible to have friends of the opposite sex without making commitments toward marriage. Believe this, and don't let pressure from others or a feeling of loss drive you into an early marriage for which you may not be ready.

True, that first person who pays special attention to you

becomes very precious. He or she may show you more love and concern than you may have felt before. Give yourself some time, though, before you promise away your own plans and life. Early marriage may mean fifty or more years of living together. Is being with that person what you really want for all that time? Don't rush—the world will still be here tomorrow. You will be, too. And that world will have changed some, and so will you.

Make Sure There Is a Future

For some, thinking about the future and dealing with the stress of being a teen can become overwhelming. And suicide is one of the greatest causes of teen death today. It's a tough subject, but it's one you must face, if not for yourself, then for your friends. While you may have the sense enough to realize that suicide never solves anything, you may need some reinforcement for others you may know now or later.

Why would a teen consider suicide? Some would say it goes back to the "raps" we raised earlier—that all teens want is entertainment, and that they cannot face life's hard realities. Most would admit that those who attempt suicide are troubled and feeling hopeless. Whatever the cause, too many teens decide there is only one way out of their problems. They consider suicide. Some go through the motions wrongly believing they won't really die. They just want to get people's attention, and they think this will do it. Some really want to commit suicide. But none of them are dealing with the right answers.

Suicide is a permanent solution to very temporary problems. It is cruel, stupid, and desperate. It hurts anyone who has cared about or loved that person.

If you ever consider committing suicide because you see no end to your problems or misery, stop a minute. Can you really believe there is no one and no group of people who will eventually care about you and truly love you for the rest of your natural life? If you answer yes, you are wrong. No one knows what the future holds. Believe that even the worst conditions will end on their own. They do. Life moves on. People and situations change. You will change. No pain or hurt is permanent. Only death is permanent. Don't let yourself—or anyone you know who may consider suicide—fall into the trap of ending temporary pain with permanent death. Don't be that stupid, and don't be that cruel. Instead, seek help and give yourself the future you deserve.

And if you see friends giving away possessions, talking of suicide, or changing their life-style and habits, do something about it. See a counselor or teacher. See anyone who can help. Don't wait. Be the caring friend who can convince a possible suicide that there *are* people who care and do not want their friends to die.

Sink or Soar?   Leaving high school can seem like jumping off a cliff. Two things can happen once you've jumped. You can sink. Or you can take off into the limitless horizon—free in your spirit and full of confidence in where the wind will take you.

How can you decide which of these two possibilities will be your future? You can, you know, influence your future just by deciding there will be nothing up ahead you cannot handle. Admit to yourself that you'll make some mistakes, probably even a big one or two, but you'll make it. You'll make it; nothing and no one will stop you! You can make your life great by accepting it and having at least a little confidence in yourself.

Don't worry yourself by looking for all the answers. Learn to love the questions because those questions can lead you to the answers. And those answers will be even better than you could ever hope for now. In time, when you are ready, all the answers will come. All you have to do is believe. Never give up on what you always have going for you—yourself, your will to be and to become, your love, and your willingness to live life to its fullest.

Rapping It Up   The future can be scary, if you let it. You may sometimes feel inadequate to handle all its demands. It can beat you down before you even give yourself a try—if you let it.

But it is possible to face the future. With a little help from counselors and national test evaluations, you can get a realistic idea of what career you would like to enter. With some understanding from the people in your life today, you can look forward to meeting new people with different ideas tomorrow. With your own goals set high and your feet on the ground, you can date and really care about someone. You can also choose to wait and promise yourself you'll be sure of someone before you give him or her the rest of your life.

Tomorrow really is an exciting place. There are no limits there, and you can be sure it holds new experiences for you. There is happiness ahead you can't even dream of now. There are people who will love the new you that is constantly becoming. The future may hold mystery and uncertainty, but it is yours to challenge and conquer—just by using all the talent, love, and determination you have.

A cliff can be the end of the road for those who think they cannot fly. However, for those who trust the wind of time and dare the risk, it can be the beginning of a wonderful new adventure. You *can* soar. You know it, and so do the people who love you. Look ahead. Dare that risk, and go for it all! Your life will only have the limits that you place on it. Brush those last traces of self-doubt away, and the world will open up to you in a thousand different ways.

Points to Ponder

1. What are some definite hopes you have for the future? Be specific.

_____

_____

_____

2. What will be the attitudes of your family members when you leave home? Why?

_____

_____

_____

_____

3. How openly can you discuss your plans for the future with your family?

_____

How much family support can you expect from them?

_____

_____

4. What qualities would you like to see in yourself at the time of your marriage?

_____

_____

_____

5. What advice would you give a friend who is afraid to face the time after graduation?

_____

_____

_____

You Bet Your Life

So how do you put all this together and make your high school years a roaring success? For starters, and finishers, believe in yourself. Through this book, you have taken an honest look at the aspects of your high school life, and at some things that may be getting in the way of your success.

You are beginning to understand that you face challenges and problems. You also, however, have uniqueness and individuality working on your side. You are good. You are intelligent enough to handle what really counts. Believe it!

Be Loyal to Yourself

One of the many talents you possess as a teenager is the ability to spot a fake miles away. You can tell when others are not being sincere, when they are caught up in some cloudy image of what they think they should be, or of what others think they should be.

Take that ability, and use it on yourself. If you know who you are, you will also know when you're not being true to yourself. You can be as great as your positive and realistic attitude allows you to be. Once you believe that, and keep that thought, no one will be able to stop you from meeting your challenges successfully.

Take All the Help You Can Get

Because society knows you are a person on the move, it has made all kinds of help available to you. Your folks, your teachers, counselors, and friends are all human, too. If you permit them to know you and share what they have with you, you can gain all the riches they offer. You can make use of their experiences, profit from their mistakes, and let them challenge you to new levels of maturity.

You can also help yourself.

Don't be afraid to take those standardized tests the counselors keep talking about. Whether geared to show career possibilities or personality traits, these tests will give you more information about yourself. They can be big boosts toward planning your life. It's true that the test findings should not be taken as absolutes, but they do provide useful clues to help you plan for the future.

Lead with Your Best Foot Forward

Getting involved in school and neighborhood activities will put you in contact with new situations. Especially if you have felt life is a colossal bore up to this point, you can begin to find some new areas for exploring your talents. Check over your interest inventory, then look at what's available in your area. Take some initiative. Investigate what's happening in your community, and soon you will find even the television reruns aren't familiar to you.

Gone, but Not Forgotten

Many teens feel they can skip a day of school here and there and still keep up with their classes. It may seem all right to stay home one day to visit with a friend or take advantage of the great weather. But truancy, or absence without permission, does more than hurt you academically. It also gives you a feeling of being on the outside, looking in. Sitting at home, browsing in a store, or walking the streets while your classmates are in school can soon make you feel apart from them—left out. If you choose to stay out of school, you may soon start feeling like a loner. You need to belong; it's part of the human condition. School, and being part of it with your friends, is where the action is for you right now.

Don't fall into the trap of taking a day off once in a while on general principle. It not only makes school officials and teachers think you are not serious about your work. It may also give you the idea you can do this in any job during your life. While missing a few days of school each semester is somewhat tolerated by schools, you'll find your future employers won't let you keep up the practice very long when you're working for them. Doing it too often might get you out on the street all right—permanently.

The Name of the Game Is Change

What is one of the surest ways to be comfortable with life and to ward off pressures? Just realize that whatever life is—it's always changing.

Many adults develop severe psychological problems because they need rock-solid security all the time. They want to get something and then hold on to it. Because of this, when a new opportunity is made available, they're afraid of trying it because they fear losing what they already have. They choose to settle for what is safe and secure, are frustrated with any change that happens, and they lead unhappy, clinging lives.

Our world is changing constantly. The job you may have when you are thirty years old may not even be invented yet. Who knows what life will be like for you or your children? No one knows what the future holds.

Scary? No. Exciting! Realizing the changes that have already happened in your life can help you understand your own personal evolutionary process. By transferring that idea to the rest of the world, and life in general, you can begin to feel comfortable with change. You can look forward with honest eagerness to all those new things that are still ahead of you.

Be flexible. Be adaptable. Be open.

Realize that what is important to you now may be totally forgotten ten years from now. Change is not something that is supposed to give you a nervous breakdown. It is a positive, exciting chance to explore new opportunities. If you can learn to make room for change in your life and welcome its challenges, you'll never turn into a narrow-minded and frustrated adult. Openness to change will lead to a stronger belief in yourself. It will also give you a more positive, hopeful outlook for the future.

There Is Nothing Stopping You!

High school is a time for learning. It is also a time for discovering your own potential. What you learn in the books is important. What you gain from knowing yourself and the way you are changing is even more important.

Sometimes teens get bogged down by all the things that are happening in their lives. They feel they have too much to handle, and they can't cope with it all. Don't let yourself get frustrated. Learn to put everything in its proper perspective by bringing your values and priorities into play. Just live each day to its fullest, and give your best. What others expect of you must be considered. However, what you expect from yourself will determine how successful you will be and how comfortable you will become with the knowledge of who you really are.

Let the things that can enrich you make your life fuller. Understand and accept the things you cannot change, and be optimistic about your ability to tackle the future. You *can* be a really great human being! If you can learn to forgive the people who may have hurt you, and realize they were acting out of their own ignorance, you can learn to love. If you can respect the humanity and individuality of others, and allow them to be themselves, you will have many friends. If you can live your own life honestly, recognizing your own limitations and your tremendous potential, you can be one of those adults whom other people look to for vision, hope, and example.

Really Rapping It Up

On your graduation day someone will hand you that precious diploma, shake your hand, and say, "Good luck!" How much luck you really need will depend on how well you succeeded in high school, and how well you use this experience as a stepping-stone to adult life.

You are not defined by your roles.

You are not limited by others' image of you.

You are the one and only, absolutely unique, and potentially terrific—you!

You can take everything that your high school years have to offer and store it neatly away in your own definition of yourself. Some of these thoughts will fall away as you mature. But how you used them when they were a part of your life will affect how you will use other new and challenging things that are to come.

Aim high, but realistically.

Live not just as a survivor, but as a successful person—a real champion at the art of living.

Enjoy. Grow. Change. You are a person on the move. So, go ahead—move on! And enjoy your future!